Let your love be like a misty rain,

coming softly but flooding the river…

For greatness of love obliterates

conventions.

~African proverbs from Madagascar and Sotho

DEDICATION

We dedicate this book to all people who seek to have a meaningful and complete relationship.

KEEP GOING

When things go wrong, as they sometimes will,

When the road you're trudging seems all uphill,
When the funds are low and the debts are high,

When you want to smile, but you have to sigh,

When cares are pressing you down a bit,
Rest if you must, but don't you quit.
Life is strange with its twists and turns,

As every one of us sometimes learns.
And many a fellow turns about,
When he might have won, had he stuck it out.
Don't give up, though the pace seems slow,

You may succeed with another go at it, another blow.
Often the goal is nearer than

It seems to a faint and faltering man.
Often the struggler has given up,
When he might have captured the victor's cup;

And he learned too late when the night came down,
How close he was to the golden crown.
Success is failure turned inside out,
The silver lining of the clouds of doubt.
And you never can tell how close you are,
It may be near when it seems afar;
So stick to the fight when you're hardest hit,
It's when things seem worst that you must not quit!
Author unknown

CONTENTS

INTRODUCTION

Staying Power: A blueprint explained
By James Williams

I am James Williams, a successful businessman, active in my community and church. I am also a divorced and proud father of three adult children. I got married when I was only 19 to my high school sweetheart. I played both sides of the fence and didn't accept my bisexuality until I realized that living a double life on the down low was not right and my choices were selfish and caused much hurt and pain. What goes around comes around is so true. I didn't want to continue hurting and using women to cover up my love and desire for men. I have been living full time as a same gender loving man for the past twenty years and have had more than my share of relationships. Some were good, and some really bad. I learned from each of my relationships and tried not to repeat the mistakes that I made in the previous ones. I have had some close calls with death and almost ruined my life more than once. Nothing too unusual happened to me.

When in grade school I had to be assisted by a lifeguard to make it out of a swimming pool. Not an emergency, but it gave me a healthy respect for fear. When I was 18 I borrowed my father's car, had to slam on the brakes, and skidded to within inches of an accident it would have been tough to explain. In my adult life I admit to having practiced unprotected sex, and yet, thank goodness I am still negative for HIV.

I have caused more pain than I am proud to admit. I wish that I could tell all my ex lovers that I am sorry for my actions. Working on this book with my partner Duane Douglas, writer and journalist Max Smith and other SGL African-American couples taught me that life is what you make it. You can live your life the way others want you to live it, or you can live a life that gives you satisfaction and completion. The most valuable lesson that this book gives is that if you don't love yourself, you can't expect someone else to love you.

Duane and I decided to write *Staying Power* while we were on our way to a movie. It was a clear, blue, beautiful Sunday in Chicago. On this day we chose just to hang out and enjoy each other. We've been in this tight relationship for over eight years. We began to reminisce about the day we met. We took inventory to discover how the same passion and excitement that attracted us to one another is still alive today. We have our ups and downs like any couple, yet we have an abiding commitment to make our relationship work. We always wondered why we have not met any other African American male couples with a "real" relationship like ours. We had other male-couple friends that didn't have the tightness in their relationships we had.

We laugh about some of the good and bad experiences we've had and we thought that perhaps we should offer a seminar to help brothers find and keep real love.

A seminar, especially for younger brothers, would be worthwhile because many of them don't have a clue about the nuances of same gender loving and romance. When we were younger there was no one around to show us an example of what goes into creating a harmonious union between two African-American men. There was no one available to help us handle coming into our own sexuality,

11

let alone anyone who could teach us the dos and don'ts of dating and maintaining romantic relationships with other African-American men.

We continued to swap war stories about our past relationships, laughing about some situations and experiences that helped us to become who we are today. We soon decided it would take a book for us truly to express our take on African-American male love.

Who are we? Friends first, lovers second, and we are two men committed to improving the quality of life for African-American men, for it is up to us to save us.

We have traveled different roads to find our meeting place in love.

My partner Duane Douglas is a part of Generation X. He is college educated, well traveled and currently enjoying his dream job in corporate America. He also has had his share of experiences dealing with brothers in his 33 years. You the reader will hear primarily my voice describe love, sexuality and romance. You also will hear the voices of numerous other brothers who gave us thoughts and ideas from their real, personal life experiences.

I called on Max Smith in Chicago to assist us in crafting this book. With his knowledge about the African-American SGL lifestyle and years of experience as a cultural, political, and community activist since 1972, there was no one else who could give this book the touch it needed to make it a reality. It is designed to present serious messages. Covering a broad range of topics, its common sense approach is sweetened with humor, and spiced with irony to make it easy for any adult to read.

What follows in *Staying Power* is a blueprint to help you construct a strong and fulfilling relationship: and/or to develop one that will last.

Staying Power is designed to bring education, wisdom, awareness, and information to the reader who wants to make good decisions and choices when it comes to finding and maintaining love. We offer stories of affirmation and encouragement. We choose not to use the word gay to describe who we are. It will appear within quotes, and occasionally to describe places and things. Black men are choosing not to be called gay, due to some negative connotations. To self-identify as being a gay man is sometimes considered too Euro-centric and too non-masculine. To soften the blow, brothers use terms like bisexual (attracted both to men and women), down low (DL, closeted, unwilling to disclose one's same gender attraction to oneself or others), family, in the life, and clockable (noticeably effeminate man or butch lesbian). The word homosexual is as antique as the word Negro. The dictionary defines the word gay as 1. Light-hearted; lively 2. Given to social pleasures 3. (noun) homosexual. To describe people, places and relationships that involve men who love or are attracted to women we use the word heterosexual, or str8.

To a lot of Black men, gay refers to being "out of the closet". To them it conjures up images of marching in the lesbian gay bisexual and transgender pride parades, wearing pink triangles or flying the rainbow flag. It puts gays in the same category of being like white men that are on the popular gay-themed television shows, which portray gay Caucasian men being flamboyant or clownlike. Brothers are not trying to be like that. African-American men have limited freedom to be openly gay and in our communities while being accepted as men. Due to the adverse affect of the term gay that society, especially the African-American community, has placed on individuals based on our sexual orientation: we have decided to use the term same gender loving (SGL). SGL is a term that is inclusive of lesbian women. It helps our communities and society become more open to the idea of SGL partnerships. When communicating with individuals that we are SGL, it forces them to look past the sexual component of our relationship. The term SGL also includes love that covers other factors of life. Few Black SGL people are clockable to heterosexuals. Yet it is easy for those of us in the life to meet family. Usually its done by cruising: using unspoken body language to put oneself on gaydar (an unspoken way of indicating interest in another SGL person). Written with a mix of humor, irony, intuition and insight, we hope you will get something useful from *Staying Power.* We welcome your feedback and look forward to having discussions with you at our future workshops on relationships coming soon to cities nationwide.

15

Peace and blessings to you.

(Please note that key cities, situations, and names of some people have been changed to protect the private identities of those people who helped this project take shape.)

WHY STAYING POWER IS NEEDED.

Nobody could tell 22-year-old J. D. Wiggins that he's not fine. Many brothers and sisters have commented on how attractive J. D. is. He spends many days at the gym, and has maintained broad shoulders, a V-shaped torso, and the physique of an Olympics–bound weightlifter. He runs five miles every morning to keep in shape, something that he continued after his time in the military. He takes pride in his ebony body, but it's the high blood pressure in his family's history that makes his daily workouts really about staying healthy. If only his choice in a man was as good as his sex appeal.

J.D. barely had two feet inside "the life" and was exploring his own sexuality when he met Robert Bancroft, age 34. They met at a Milwaukee automobile dealership where Robert worked as a salesman.

Although J. D. often fantasized about having sex with other men, he never had found the courage to actually go through with it. His torrid fantasies were just sexual thoughts he'd masturbate to frequently as a teenager, which carried over well into his days as an enlisted U. S. Army soldier. Now out of Uncle Sam's grip as an honorably discharged veteran, J. D. found himself thinking about men every day and every night.

He was not trying to brand himself gay, even though it had been four years since he had sex with a woman. He doesn't walk with limp wrists, talk in falsetto and is in no way clockable. But he knows that his strong attraction for men is not a passing phase. That fact became quite evident when he met Robert while shopping for a new car. Robert is a smooth talker always on the prowl for young and fresh meat. The product of a Puerto Rican mother and an Italian-American father, he had a notorious reputation for being a seasoned Don Juan – often bedding the lovers of his close friends and associates. To add insult to injury, Robert also was an ex-felon who served several years in prison for credit card fraud and check deception. Many of Robert's friends attributed his devious and manipulative

17

ways to the fact that his mother abandoned him. She left him to grow up as a ward of the state in a series of foster homes. Eventually adopted as a teenager, Robert fell prey to sexual abuse at the hands of his new father.

With striking looks and a persuasive personality, Robert was a charmer many found difficult to refuse, as J. D. would soon find out. Robert often found himself greeting many of the Black men who came into the dealership and it was no different when J. D. walked along the rows of shiny new vehicles to find his new ride. The two men exchanged a long stare before Robert walked up to J. D. who had refocused his attention on a burly black Buick Rendezvous. Between the handshake that lasted ten seconds longer than str8 men would shake hands, and the long stares the two men exchanged J. D. could tell he was being cruised on gaydar and quickly asked for an auto finance application. When Robert called a couple days later to let J. D. know he was approved for the car loan, he suggested that the two get together for a round of beers at a nearby bar to celebrate the news. J. D. obliged. That evening was the start of a rocky two-year relationship. Within three months, J. D. had moved into Robert's apartment. Within six months, the romantic bliss had worn off. Problems started to creep into J. D's infatuation affair with Robert that not only included knock-down fights, but Robert's constant mind games, stalking and his frequent recording of J. D's personal telephone conversations. It became so stressful, J. D. found himself turning to brandy, scotch and gin to find solace. Soon, plans to finish his business college curriculum ended up being deferred to a later time.

He presently became so caught up dealing with the effects of Robert's insecurity and his manipulative, possessive and controlling ways that he wound up following in his senior lover's footsteps: committing bank fraud through credit card and check deception.

The actions led him to a nine-month stint in the county jail and three years of probation.

Yet, J.D. still hadn't had enough. Despite the turmoil of their two-year relationship, he still couldn't shake the feelings of love, caring and sympathy that lived inside his heart for Robert, his first male lover.

After his release from county jail and a felony on his record, J.D. tried on several occasions to jump-start his love affair with Robert. At the time of this book's writing, J. D. finds himself still having a very hard time letting go. While the pair no longer lives together, they still date and frequently have sex with each other.

J. D's story is not an isolated incident.

His story transcends age as many Black bisexuals and men who love men, despite our stage of physical and mental maturity, can relate to the feelings of having unrealistic expectations of the "perfect" relationship. Then too soon, we look up and find ourselves in an emotional jam--- compromising our values, core beliefs and forsaking all we once held sacred.

There is a better way and it's not found in a liquor bottle, in the denial of reality, or in mindless, thoughtless, anonymous sex. It's not even found in the company of our parents and caregivers: to whom we could run, in our most needy times of distress.

The answer lies within us, and how we choose to determine how we negotiate our way through love.

Although the exact number of SGL African-American couples living together in the USA is unclear and difficult to track. African-American men are well represented in the approximately 3.8 million unmarried-partner households in this country. This is according to numbers compiled by the US Census Bureau in the year 2000.

Some African-American men are in happy and healthy relationships, but many like J. D. and Robert are knee-deep in domestic violence, drama, addiction and confusion.

Staying Power provides slices of information on just what it takes to weather the storms of love from the perspective of African-American men. We offer a way to stay true to your love without becoming lost and dishonoring who you are as a man who already is traveling a rough and bumpy road in this world. There are some ground rules we operate by.

No one can misuse you without your permission. Yet no one can make you happy if you despise the very essence of your spirit as a man who has an attraction to men. Only God can give you Staying Power. God, Allah, Buddha, or who or whatever you identify as your Higher Power is always right on time, supplying tools we need to rise up and live life well.

It is designed to be a workbook and a self-help interactive guide.

May you learn, grow and love to your fullest potential.

Chapter 1

<u>To Thine Own Self Be True</u>
"Look at the man in the mirror"

"If you know the beginning well,
The end will not trouble you."

~Wolof Proverb

"I need a man with a C-A-R, a J-O-B and I prefer one with a H-O-M-E, but he definitely needs an A-P-T," says Reggie Daniels, a 55-year-old, African-American medical technician from Indianapolis.

"So you want somebody with a car, a job and you prefer someone with a home, but what is an A-P-T?" we asked.

"Apartment, baby!" says Reggie.

"I don't want no man who's still livin' at home with momma, out on the street like a damned transient, and honey, he can't stay at my villa. Oh no, no, no, no, no, no, no, chile!"

"Cause when the brotha' fucks up, he can go right on about his business," says Reggie. "This diva don't do the live-in-lover thang.....once bitten, twice shy, OKAY!"

Next, walks in Mark Stevens, a banker from Hartford, Connecticut.

His mahogany-brown, finely manicured hand reaches deep inside his tan Coach attaché as he pulls out the controversial magazine.

The cover reads: "From Schools to Jobs, Black Women Are Rising Much Faster Than Black Men. What It Means for Work, Family and Race Relations."

"The article reveals that brothers are lagging behind, we as a group are fuckin' up and the women say they may end up living alone because they cannot find suitable men to marry or be in relationships with," says Mark.

"I feel for the sistahs, I mean they got all that good pussy and still can't find the right brotha'."

"But I want them to feel my pain as a fairly young, professional, black-gay man."

"At 35 years-old, I once had thoughts of having a family, with children and a life-long companion, but as the years go by sometimes I do wonder how realistic this is."

"I'm trying to stay positive, but I'm not going to settle, because I have standards.... I go by occupation, education and transportation.... my man needs all three."

"That's not asking for too much, is it?"

• • •

"A Black gay relationship with two men?" asked 26-year-old sanitation worker Marvin Hastings, of St. Louis. "I just don't think it can work."

"It's not designed for two men to be together that way...believe me I know because I've tried."

Marvin, who shares a resemblance to the type of brother you see in popular R & B groups. Tall, dark skinned, sexy eyes and just 100 percent fine, says he's been romantically involved with more than a dozen men in his adult life.

"All of the relationships I've had probably lasted a total of six months to a year.... The men are either too needy, too possessive, too jealous, too whorish or too gay."

"What's too gay?" we asked.

"Too flamin' for me," says Marvin. "If I wanted a woman,

I would go and get me one."

Utterly dissatisfied with dating, casual sex and playing both ends against the middle, dealing with both men and women-- he's now taken himself off the market as a 26th birthday present to himself.

"I can do badly, all by myself," he says.

"So, what is it that you're looking for, Marvin?"

"That's a good question, I don't know what I want."

"That's why it's probably best I'm not out there now lookin' for somebody, I need to get to know Marvin better first."

Reggie Daniels, Mark Stevens and Marvin Hasting may vary in age, live in different parts of the country, and work in different environments, but they share something in common. They are men trying to navigate the waters of love and what it means to be both Black and SGL in America.

There's a Negro spiritual that goes:

"Nobody told me the road would be easy, but I don't believe He brought me this far to leave me."

Many of us who are Black and SGL in this country can relate to those words. We have become all too familiar with the frustration, loneliness, and hurt oftentimes associated with living a life that's unconventional at best, yet as real as the rising Sun, and just as valid as anyone else's life.

For just as there is great frustration, pain and hurt, there is an equal abundance, if not more, of joy, peace and comfort in being what others fear, hate or sometimes just do not understand.

Reggie, Mark, Marvin and others in the family may not always be aware of just how powerful their presence is in a world that would rather have them live and dwell in the shadows of society. Prejudiced people can barely tolerate them as individuals; let alone accept the idea that they actually have aspirations of building romantic unions and relationships with other like-minded men.

Some lesbian, gay, bisexual and transgender activists say the idea of two Black men loving each other is revolutionary. After all we live in a nation in which about 11,000 Black men shoot and kill other Black men every year.

However the author James, of *Staying Power*, chooses to agree with *B-Boy Blues* author James Earl Hardy, who once said

"Who has decided that my loving someone, who is a reflection of myself is a revolutionary act?.....What evidence do they have to prove it is, and if it's a revolutionary act, what is a Black SGL man to do if he can't love another Black man and, by extension, love himself?"

A Black man loving another Black man is less a revolutionary act and more a natural fact of everyday life. A fact of life lost on herterosextuals who do not see the silent, closeted and invisible who make up a majority of the SGL community.

29

This book gives sensible voice to the validity of the SGL experience and delivers a message that it's possible to create peace, harmony and balance in these relationships. It only makes sense that it is indeed a challenge to maintain such a relationship. To be of African descent and also same gender loving can at times require an approach to life of defiant opposition to historic racist and homophobic oppressions. In other words, living a quiet revolution.

The keys to harmony and balance have everything to do with the standards and the foundation on which the relationship is built.

Before two people are joined in a romantic sense, they are each two unique individuals on a journey of self-discovery as seen with Reggie, Mark and Marvin.

Did you read how each man briefly explained sound bite versions of their individual standards for choosing a partner and companion?

Standards are important to establishing relationship

ground rules and principles: they serve as a guide into the mind, body and spirit of an individual.

Relationship standards are the boundaries a person defines and constructs as a way to achieve the kind of romantic intimacy, bliss and joy we think our relationships have the potential to reach.

For Reggie, it is important for his potential lover to have a degree of independence. He does not want a man who cannot stand on his own two feet.

Mark wants someone who is on his same professional level. Someone who is intelligent and can provide him with intellectual stimulation is critical. Marvin desires the kind of guy who is not the stereotypical homosexual. His ultimate catch is extremely masculine: a man many people may never detect as same gender loving from outward appearances. Standards, based upon individual emotional, spiritual and physical needs, are important to establishing relationship values and principles. They serve as a guide into the mind, body and spirit of each partner. Some men place brains

31

before beauty, others will not settle for anything less than financial security, while many just want steamy hot sex.

In the end, we have to live comfortably with our own selves and what works for one person may not work for you.

The intimacy of a private union shared by two individuals requires boundaries that work for both partners.

Relationship standards are the boundaries we define for ourselves in order to achieve a desired level of compatibility with our lovers. As we grow and move along life's journey, some of our standards may change. This may cause us to reprioritize what we once held as primary on our dating wish lists. We've encountered friends who once lived for the freedom to have sex with whomever they want without attached emotional strings, only to find out later that they are ready to settle down and make a serious emotional investment with someone. Change is a natural part of life. The tricky part is determining standards for an unconventional relationship between two men. While many heterosexual couples often enter into a relationship with an expectation that love will last for an eternity, many SGL men do not share that same concept of permanency for our romantic encounters.

Marvin clearly demonstrates this thought-process when he makes the statement:

"It's not designed for two men to be together that way."

This can become a self-fulfilling prophecy. A way to stop that kind of negative thinking is first to come to terms with your inner spirit, as a Black same gender loving man. Start developing a plan for your own life. First get to know just who you are. Understand through introspection what you believe in. Then be honest with yourself about how and why faith motivates you: whether it is faith in God, in humanity, in nature or in a desire for money. Finally accept and acknowledge the fears that hold you back. Do you fear being the center of attention should you become successful? Do you fear the challenge of moving outside your familiar routine, beyond your comfort zone? There is an old adage that misery loves company. Can you motivate yourself into a constant willingness to think affirmative thoughts? Are you able to see the glass as half full? Do you have the self-discipline to say upbeat, optimistic and cheerful comments to your partner on a daily basis? Will your partner think of you as his motivator and as the one he can count on to give him the encouragement he needs when the going gets tough? There are many people suffering from emotional depression, anxiety and fear about their sexuality. Many times the depression and anxiety is obvious in a person. There are many men who can publicly mask their self-hatred, but as you get to know them over time in their intimate emotional zone, it becomes obvious. It can manifest itself as speaking out persistent pessimism or as acting out violence, or self-defeating behavior. One friend we knew took out a student loan. We congratulated him for getting good grades in student nursing classes. Then, his self-hatred crept in. Just one week before final exams he would have aced, he defeated himself by dropping out of school. He got drunk when he heard all his classmates passed the exam and earned their nursing certificate. He hated the thought of being successful. He had heard his father call him a good-for-nothing sissy all his life, and he let that tape replay in his mind again and again and again. What a terrible waste of human potential! And he's still repaying that loan. It is an understatement to say that at times it can be very challenging to love or make another person happy who is not fully comfortable living inside their own skin.

FIRST THINGS FIRST! GET TO KNOW WHO YOU ARE:
When you have a firm sense of the moral compass that guides your thoughts, motivations and actions, you can then chart a clear course of forward action for your world. You can set a tone that partially determines the events that occur in your life and the people who may be attracted into your sphere of personal energy.

It can be a battle receiving love when a cloud of confusion and turmoil is cast over the head of a person with sexual identity issues.

Some people don't fully know they have a problem with their sexual identity until they are intimately confronted or involved with someone who begins to mirror the parts of themselves they hate.

The questions are as complex as the answers. African-American SGL men have had many opportunities to define who we are here in America. Our freedom of speech, of religious belief, of the free press, etc. is greater than at any time in history. It is greater than in most other countries. Yet, even into the 21st Century, you see some of the vestiges of "slavery ways" impacting the African-American male psyche. Dr. Naim Akbar has written a book about the long-term psychological after-effects of slavery. They include internal turmoil, self-hatred, and repressive mentality. You can see it in the infamous Morehouse incident of Black-male bashing at an all Black-male University. Two students were in a shower room. One, who had misplaced his glasses, looked into a shower stall thinking he heard his roommate in there. The student who was looked at became enraged, claiming the other man was making a sexual advance on him. His over-reaction to being merely looked at, was to get a baseball bat, bring it into the shower, and to crack the skull of the man who had lost his glasses. You can see it in the famous cases of Kobe Bryant, Mike Tyson, and O. J. Each a previously admired and respected celebrity, behaving too recklessly to be role models for youth. Need we say more--- all the rappers practicing misogyny and getting beautiful Black women to be just babies mamas. How else to explain a father's running away from the responsibility of child rearing and support over 18 years? Can they ever respect the man in their mirror? Will a bisexual in denial over sexual identity issues ever admit that making and abandoning a baby does not prove his manhood? Baltimore-based counselor Henry Westray, LCSW, says a person's comfort level with his sexuality can make or break a relationship.

"One of the things a man must ask himself before getting involved with another man on any level--- whether sexual, dating or if they desire a long-term union--- is how openly gay do I want to be in my personal and professional life?" asks Westray. "Answering this question can save a lot of emotional grief."

Answering the question also requires a commitment to be truthful to one's self and may require time as men learn how to grow into our own emotional and psychological maturity.

Another area that is cause for reflection is the degree to which a man feels comfortable verbally communicating needs, desires and thoughts.

We will give you our "recipe." Begin with the assertive and affirming WORDS we use. Those words serve to reflect a strong positive IMAGE we declare ourselves to be. That good image manifests itself with DEEDS consistent with the vigor and power of a made-up mind. True, there are historical underpinnings to be considered as it relates to the bio-psycho-social aspects of those Black men who identify as same gender loving. But now and into the future it's time that we must exercise the KWANZAA principles of unity, self-determination, collective work and responsibility, cooperative economics, purpose, creativity and faith to establish our respective places in society.

Further progress toward greater self-disclosure can vary according to pre-existing attitudes in your particular family, community, the church, the political environment and the sense of personal security you feel given the national economy.   In our patriarchal society, where strength is revered, many men tend to shy away from talking about our "feelings." The belief is that doing so makes a man soft and weak.

Sometimes a man's comfort level with communication is not so much rooted in sexist stereotypes, but has everything to do with the parental and/or care-giving environment in which he was nurtured.

There are many parents and caregivers that expect children to be seen and not heard.

Men nurtured in these environments may not have built a strong level of confidence in expressing themselves in their childhood years because they may have been reprimanded for voicing their thoughts and opinions, which may have been perceived as a challenge to the parent or care-giver's authority.

Many black parents pride themselves for not taking any back talk from their children; and, what may be perceived as such may land a kid a quick pop in the mouth or a sharp tongue lashing as a result of so-called "disrespecting" authority.

No matter the reason, a poor communicator will have a tough time in any relationship. Ongoing, clearly worded, and very directly spoken communication every day is required to build a solid relationship. We'll discuss communication techniques later in another chapter, however other personal considerations a man must determine for himself before opening his heart to another can be found in our: *Staying Power Self-Assessment Worksheet.*

THE STAYING POWER SELF-ASSESSMENT WORKSHEET

A man who aimlessly goes through life without guiding principles of action is a fool going nowhere fast. No one wants to board a ship without first knowing its destination. To measure your personal code of conduct, determine where you stand on the following: *What three codes of conduct motivate my actions?*

_____

_____

_____

What three material items do I value more than any others?

_____

_____

_____

With three months to live, and good health, what would I do? _____

_____

_____

41

Am I shy or do I like being the center of attention?

_____

_____

_____

What three things should somebody say about me when I die? _____

_____

_____

What are my fears? _____

_____

_____

What brings me joy? _____

_____

_____

What makes me angry? _____

_____

_____

What are my personal strengths? _____

_____

_____

_____

How do I define love? _____

_____

_____

_____

How do I expect someone to show love to me? _____

_____

_____

_____

What are my thoughts about sex? _____

_____

_____

_____

How do I handle feelings of jealousy, stress and
frustration? _____

_____

_____

_____

Why am I relationship material? _____

_____

_____

_____

How do I react when someone hurts or disrespects me?

_____

_____

_____

*Can I truly forgive a person, who has committed a
wrong against me?* _____

_____

_____

*Do I handle disputes with my fists or can I talk things
out?* _____

_____

_____

What do I bring to the table for a potential mate? _____

_____

_____

_____

What do I expect a mate to bring to the table in my
relationship? _____

_____

_____

How open with my lifestyle and sexuality do I want to be
in my professional life? _____

_____

_____

_____

Am I a family-oriented person? _____

_____

_____

_____

How selfish am I? _____

_____

_____

_____

What are my attitudes about money and material
possessions? _____

_____

_____

What principles do I try to live by on a day to day basis?

_____

_____

_____

Take time to ask yourself these questions. Call on yourself to develop a personal code of conduct. When you discuss these questions and your answers with your current or future partner, you will learn new things about him, and he will learn more about you, and a deeper understanding develops through this deliberate effort to foster in-depth communication.

Chapter 2

WHEN HE'S MARRIED OR HAS A GIRLFRIEND

"YOU ARE A FOOL"

"A deaf man may not have heard the thunder,
but he surely will see the rain   ~Mali Proverb

Being involved with a married man or one with a girlfriend is a common mistake many SGL men make. In fact, some men find the married and the attached more attractive than others. They feel that they can deal with them on their own terms: when they want, how often they want, however they want, simply because they are married or with someone else.

It is often easier to send them back to their female partner, who has all the social props anyway. So, men shrug and say to themselves: let his wife or let his girlfriend deal with his issues.

You are a fool if:
A man is honest enough to tell you he's married or has a girlfriend and you still want to be with him! The sole nature of your relationship with him is just a sexual hook-up, and you know he's not going to leave his female partner for you.
The brother on the down low will not speak to you, if he sees you on the street: or will not acknowledge you in public. He tells you up-front how you better not step to him outside of the sexual relationship and the only time you see him is when he wants to have sex.

48

He will not give you his real name or any information about himself such as where he lives or works. Putting up with this kind of disrespectful behavior cheapens you. Many of us have had dealings with this type of down-low brother. He is a man who loves having sex with other men, an MSM, who is only in it for the sex. They are prized catches as their strong masculinity and straight-acting ways melt the hearts of many in "the family." Many of us have been hurt when a relationship like this spins out of control, as was the case for Duane. The lesson here is very clear. When you let your little head, or his little head, make your love life decisions then you are a fool, and he is a fool too. If you love him, and he has told you that he loves you, then he needs to let his wife go. Set her free, free from his lying. If you are willing to share him with a female, and he has told you that he is not planning on leaving his family or his woman for you, then you have endorsed the behavior of men who are having a devastating impact on sisters around the world.

Duane's long-term trysting experience with a married man:

49

I was in a relationship with a married man for more than seven years. He was attractive to me because he was already in a relationship. We all want what we can't have, right? It's kind of like a gamble or challenge. You want to see if you can win the lottery prize. I met David Gentry at a local department store. It was the smell of his cologne that made me notice him as he was looking at a few watches, while I waited to get mine fixed. We felt a vibe with one another in a heartbeat. His quick wit had me in stitches as he made fun of the sales clerk behind the counter having a very bad hair day. Soon we found ourselves talking about what brought us out shopping and that's when I felt he might be family. So I tested him. When he reached to shake my hand, I made sure to scratch the inside of his hand --- one of the insider ways to identify family. He was smooth about it and followed suit. As we talked David's charm and handsome looks had me open up as he told me all the things I wanted to hear: that I'm sexy, smart and sophisticated. He was halfway honest from the jump and told me he was married. We exchanged phone numbers, although, I found out later he wrote down a fake last name. He intimated it would be best to call him during the weekends while his wife was away. I respected his wishes. David also explained how he was not very happy in his marriage. Said he didn't like the way his wife had put on 40 pounds since their wedding, said she did not want to go out on the town anymore and so he was contemplating a divorce. As far as I was concerned that was his problem, not mine. A few days later I called the house and we talked for a couple of hours. It was as if we'd known each other for years. Before hanging up we decided to meet the next day during my lunch hour when his wife was at work.

When I arrived at his house, I was extremely nervous. In the back of my mind I kept thinking David's wife could come home any second. The thought made me jump at the slightest sound in the house. Their cat jumped onto the couch where we were sitting, and scared me to death. David motioned for me to come closer to him, and before I knew it we were deep kissing and fondling each other. Next, our clothes were on the floor and we were having sex. Our passionate sex developed into weekly get-togethers and soon we found ourselves hanging out with each other at the movies, park, and sporting events. On one outing I met his wife. He introduced me to her as a high school friend. She told me she was glad David met an old buddy that he could do things with. (If only she knew all the things we were doing!) When I decided to take a job in a different part of the city, I found myself looking for a new apartment. David suggested I temporarily move in with him and his wife while I searched for a new place. First I hesitated, then agreed, thinking the set-up would last no more than a month. Once I moved in, I noticed a change in David. He became more controlling and he wanted to know my every move when I was not with him. I desperately wanted to please him because I believed he loved me. I even ended up abandoning plans to get my own place because he convinced me it would be cheaper to stay with him and his wife than to be out on my own. I never had been involved with a man before in this way so I didn't know what to expect. Except that friends had told me that many Black women are socialized to accept any and all decisions a husband makes. Many Black women are emotionally blind to the presence of SGL and bisexual men. As time went on it became clear he was not going to divorce his wife. I started to feel guilty about living under the circumstances. David's manipulation caused me to withdraw and I soon dropped my friends and family because I was so ashamed of what I was doing.

We began to fight each other and that was when I knew it was time to go. Dealing with the pain of all that made stress became very great. Too often we would have to abruptly stop sex and scramble to get dressed right away upon hearing her car pull up into the driveway. I had this weird thought that she deliberately neglected to replace the noisy muffler on that little red Plymouth Neon so she could be sure we would hear her arriving back home. That way she could maintain her state of denial, and never risk catching us in the act. Sometimes I'd have to force a smile and be pleasant with her, when I really wasn't feeling it. After the midnight hour I often could hear David and his wife making passionate love through the bedroom wall and I couldn't stand it. I had to decide enough is enough! So I left him. I still have nightmares about the way he treated me. I have flashbacks of the mental and emotional hell he put me through.

This story is a perfect example of how something that started off in a sexual way led into a complicated web of lies and deceit. David was a master of mendacity.

Some of us can't handle only having a sexual relationship with a man. Some want to advance it to the emotional level: convincing ourselves and actually believing that in time the brother will come around. A friend of James and me in Los Angeles knew he was a married man's piece on the side. Yet and still he found himself falling in love with the hot rod and couldn't let go. He was so open for this brother that he found a way to ingratiate himself to the guy's family --- developing good relations with the man's wife and children in hopes of spending more time with this brother. After the guy told him that he no longer wanted to be on the down low and he planned to dedicate all of his life, time and attention to his family, our Los Angeles friend went into a deep depression. Now if you want to go through this type of hell and know that in the end you are the one who will end up by yourself, all alone, starting over again, then you remember what I said earlier in this chapter.....

What goes around comes around. FOOL!

Look up the word adultery in your dictionary. It applies to you. Letting a married man have his cake and eat it too has contributed to the sharp increases of HIV infection among African-American women. This is because a man who has been married for years is not going to start wearing a condom upon starting an affair with you. How would he explain to his wife the need to suddenly stop having unprotected sex? Black women represent one of the fastest growing groups of new HIV cases as a result of their husbands and lovers having unprotected sex with numerous men and women's contact with IV drug users.

A message from a sister to the men who know their sexual partners have wives or girlfriends.

Dear Brothers;

I found out that my man, the love of my life, the father of my son, was having sex with men when I saw him one day coming out of an apartment building on the west side of the city. I was with a co-worker and we had to make a visit to one of our clients. I saw my man laughing and joking as he was coming out of the building with this brother who I did not know. I saw them get into the brother's dark blue 1999 Ford Thunderbird and drive away. I later found out that he was in a relationship with this brother. I found this out because I took the brother's Illinois Land of Lincoln plate number off the brother's T-bird, and ran a check on it. (Through a friend who works for the DMV) and from information, I found out where he lived, his name and other important facts. I went to his apartment and knocked on the door...yes I did. I was mad as hell and wanted to know why my man was with him when he had told me he was going to be busy all day at work. He answered, saying something about the "T" on my man's bird, but we had a long talk. He didn't know anything about me. I told him to call my husband and invite him over. He did, and when Mark showed up, he got the surprise of his life. I was sitting there, serious as a heart attack, and both of us confronted him. There was nothing he could say. In the end he lost his lover and me. Brothers, please just leave women alone. It is not fair for you to hurt and use us to cover up your sexual orientation. If you are bisexual, then let women have the informed choice of if we want to deal with you. Please don't make this decision for us. It is not right. And it is not fair to us. Think of your sister or any important women in your life. If it happened to them, how would you feel?

Submitted by:

Ms – I'm not going to be used again as your front!!

Chapter 3

FREE WILL
"GOD'S GREATEST GIFT"

"Too much fear creates slavery"

~Swahili proverb

We are all born with free will. Among all living things on the planet Earth, we humans can think and reason. The exercising of rational thought allows us to control emotions, and to manage and pre-plan how to deal with biological impulses. Whether we realize it or not, we all have the ability to make our own decisions. A man is going to do exactly what he wants, when he wants and how he wants.

With this freedom thousands and thousands of choices we make every hour and every day add up to a life lived. Are we to try and take that freedom of choice away from another individual? No! Once you realize that, it makes everything that you have no control over easier to accept, especially when it comes to fellow human beings.

I learned this the hard way. For all my adult life I have always tried to control other people. I tried to control my children well into their adult lives, and it was a constant battle. When I tried to control my former partners, I always found myself stressed out, because grown men always do what they want to do.

My last serious relationship ended, because I tried to control him. After that, I told myself that any relationship that I get into would have free will as its foundation. There are multiple aspects to having free will in a relationship. One benefit to it is that both individuals are free to make decisions without asking permission. This freedom also gives each person total control of his life, so it can be lived as he chooses. Another benefit is that you learn to build trust in your partner. Complete honesty by both mates is required. Mutual respect is created.

My partner Duane was not used to this type of freedom. In his past relationships, he had been controlled: his decisions were not his, but his partner's. He was not allowed to choose his clothes, friends, what he ate, where he partied, when he could go to church or how much time he could spend with his family. He was used to having another man tell him when he would have sex, how he would have sex, and how long it would last. He had no say in any area of his life. He once told me that his lover would make him masturbate if he came home late so he could see if he had had sex while he was out. Duane's friend knew that if he didn't produce a lot of semen, then he must have had sex, and a verbal beat-down would follow. Could you live your life under the control of a dictator? Under the watchful eyes of another man who felt seriously that he owned you, and that his decisions were your decisions?

Having free will was new to him, and it took him a long time to get used to it. But once he did, it opened his life up to a whole, new, free world: a world in which he controlled his decisions, a world in which he didn't have to ask anyone for anything. It was his choice, his personal freedom. Give your partner free will. For as long as your love shall last it will serve to reduce stress and pressure. Exercise self-control, self-discipline and adherence to the ground rules of your relationship, in thought, word and deed.

MICHAEL'S SPIRITUAL JOURNEY:

A good friend of mine, Michael is a 40 year-old brother born in Petersburg, Virginia with a quiet self-confident demeanor at all times. He told me about how he came to love and accept being both SGL and Christian:

Ever since I was young, my religious family taught me to have reverence for the Spirit of the Almighty. I learned that the most important part of a person is the soul. It is the soul that governs our thoughts, desires and passions. Having grown up in the church; and having heard every Sunday that "the soul that sinneth shall surely die" helped me realize the importance of getting my soul "right with the Lord". At a point I had to come to grips with my SGL being. I am God's creation, made in God's image and likeness. I memorized the scripture John 3:16 in Sunday school, "God so loved the people of the world that he gave his only begotten son so that whosoever shall believe in him shall not perish but have everlasting life". My soul rejoices to believe that "whosoever" most definitely includes SGL folk. If people were to follow the Golden Rule, to "Love your neighbor as you love yourself," the world would have greater peace and harmony. I connect with the creator through the medium of fervent diligent prayer. At the end of the day I hope that the spirits of SGL folks can be uplifted. I have chosen to leave a church in which SGL folks were condemned from the pulpit, and joined one where we are affirmed. That critical choice

63

made a world of difference in how well I feel about myself and about others. What helped me most was a reference book written by Harvard University author and theologian Rev. Peter J. Gomes. The Good Book: Reading The Bible With Mind And Heart is a well-rounded perspective on how human prejudices shaped moral attitudes.

"If you constantly seek the validation of others, you will often be disappointed. Yet when you live, and love and act in each moment with the best that you have to give, the real value you create can never be diminished."
~Ralph Marston

Chapter 4

WHY DOESN'T HE LISTEN TO ME?
"BLAH, BLAH, BLAH"

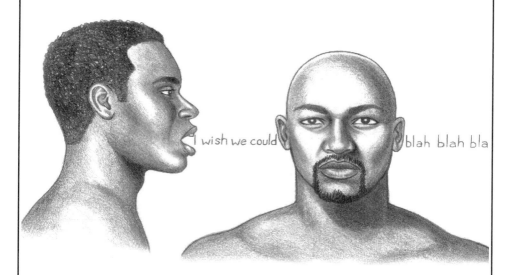

Talking with another is loving one another.
~Kenyan proverb

When I first met Frank, my ex, we would talk on the phone for hours everyday and every night we would have marathon conversations. I would lie in the bed with my favorite jazz CD playing, some candles lit, and dressed in nothing but the sheet wrapped around me.

We would talk about everything. And I hung on to every word Frank said to me. We would talk about our goals, families, and what we wanted from a lover. That subject was always 90% of our conversations. Love. I remember on a couple of long calls; I fell asleep with the phone at my ear, because I didn't want to hang up. Truly neither one of us wanted to be the first to say good night. Sometimes he would sing me a song or I would be cooking and he would share cooking recipes. I would laugh at him for trying to tell me how to cook. And he would tell me something he was cooking was all-good. Then we would get to talking on the phone, until he smelled that tasty treat burning on the stove down in the kitchen. We would be so involved in conversation that nothing else mattered.

Those were wonderful days and I miss that. We never had

a break down in communication. He knew what I was thinking, and could tell when I was not feeling good. He would even know when I was holding back on something important.

Eight months into the relationship things started to change. We no longer talked to each other. I was sharing my life with my friends, and he would be on line or sending e-mail to his best friend in Philadelphia.

How we got to this point I do not know. What happened to the open dialogue, the sharing of information that was so important? One evening while having dinner, I asked him, why is it that every time when I say something is wrong with our relationship, it goes in one ear and out the other? Why is it that when I want to share with you something about my life, my health, my feelings, my job or my love for you, you just sit there and stare at me. You give me no feedback or any type of reaction, good or bad? What's up with you? Are we now living in a different world?

He laid down the newspaper that he was reading.

He looked directly into my eyes he said something that made me think. "You act like you are not interested in anything that is going on in my world. You are so busy talking about what's going on with you, in your world that you stopped listening to me. Since you are so busy talking you are not listening. So, I stopped telling you anything." This shocked me, and there was nothing I could say. He was right. I had gotten so caught up in my stuff that I didn't think that much about him. It was not about him. Everything was all about me. From that day forward I used my two ears more than my one mouth. He and I again would share and talk with each other (not at each other) like we did in the earlier stages of our relationship. I learned that if I wanted him to listen to me, I had to listen to him. I vowed never to let communication break down again due to my being overly selfish about conversation subject matter.

Chapter 5

DEFENSE OF SGL
RELATIONSHIPS ACTS
"TAKING CARE OF YOUR BUSINESS"

Knowledge is better than richs

~Cameroon proverb

On Thursday June 26, 2003 the United States Supreme Court ruled in favor of an African-American man Tyron Garner and his Caucasian partner John Lawrence. If the case had been before the Supreme Court before June 1967, these guys would have been in double trouble. Until the mid-1960's, in many states interracial relationships were illegal. Houston police, responding to a false report of illegal firearms in the home of John Lawrence, entered his home. The cops caught him in the act of having sex with Tyron Garner. Under the Texas "Homosexual Conduct" sodomy law, the couple was arrested, held in jail, and charged a hefty fine. That law, and all other USA sodomy laws, were declared an unconstitutional invasion of privacy by the Supreme Court.

The first sodomy law was enacted under King Henry VIII, in England in 1533. Similar laws dating from 18th Century colonial America and still on the books in 13 mainly southern states also were voided June 26, 2003.

Despite what Thomas Jefferson and George Washington said about "life, liberty, and the pursuit of happiness," they and most of their peers owned slaves. The traditional

70

family value to them was about $2500, the retail purchase price of one African-American family of two adults and two children. For about 100 years since the 13th Amendment to the U. S. Constitution ended slavery in 1865, same gender love was called "the love that dared not to speak its name."

In 1963 Black gay activist Bayard Rustin's work inspired a renewal of the expansion of civil liberties with his successful organizing of the August 28, 1963 March on Washington D. C. where Dr. Martin Luther King gave his famous "I Have A Dream" speech.

In June 1967 the U. S. Supreme Court declared interracial relationships legal. On June 28, 1969 transgender patrons of color at the Stonewall Inn, a gay bar in New York City, rioted against police harassment and brutality. The Stonewall revolt marks the start of the modern LGBT liberation movement. A little-known fact of Black History Month is that an African-American woman cast the deciding vote in East Lansing, Michigan in February 1973 to enact the first municipal gay rights anti-discrimination ordinance. In 1982 Wisconsin became the first of several states to outlaw discrimination against SGL people in employment and public accommodations.

By fighting and winning their case at the federal level, Lawrence and Garner secured privacy rights and made it possible for other activists to move on to seek the right to have SGL relationships recognized by United States, as they are in some provinces of Canada. In turn that opens the possibility for SGL folks to adopt children, to get expanded employment opportunities and benefits, to get hospital visitation rights, naturalization rights: in essence, full citizenship.

YOU HAVE TO BE VISIBLE TO BE RECOGNIZED.

We think that if you are going to be in a committed relationship and live together you need to put your affairs in order. Whether or not the state you live in legislates; domestic partnerships, civil unions, or same gender marriage, you should utilize legal options already available.

We have heard the horror stories of how the families of a SGL couple fought over the estate when one of the brothers died. Because they did not tell anyone about their relationship or have a will that spelled out the transfer of property, the surviving partner ended up with nothing. If the families don't know, then what are they supposed to do? Stand back and let you claim that he loved you, and that all of the furniture, cars and money that was in his name and not in your name belongs to you because that is the way it was? Wrong, bro! You will get your feelings hurt. Then you will find yourself in a shelter for the homeless! A close friend of ours told us recently that at the funeral of a friend, the lover of the deceased was not invited to have any say about the arrangements. He was asked to get out of the apartment of the deceased and not to touch anything or take anything. The mother of the deceased called the police the day she told him to get out, to make sure that he left with nothing, not even his own clothes. Because the two of them lived in the closet and never shared their relationship with anyone, the family assumed that the lover of the deceased, in a relationship for four years, was a roommate: and he was treated like a roommate. Even family members of the deceased who whispered that he was rumored to be a fag, kept their gossiping mouths shut and allowed the lover to be treated like a dog. It was sad because during the services the lover sat in the back of the church, and was not allowed to say anything at the funeral. None of their friends were involved in any of the planning. Instead they quietly celebrated the life of the deceased at a private gathering far away from the family. The lover lost everything. He had to start over from scratch. But the one thing he lost the most was that one last chance to say good-bye to his partner, so the world could see how much in love they were.

What you have to do is to cover your assets. Both of you need to go see a lawyer sensitive to SGL issues, and have a will drawn up that states what you want the family and everybody else to know about your relationship, and what your lover is entitled to. Allow him to be the executor of your estate, and vice-versa. Do not be closeted with your attorney. If your lawyer cannot handle having a SGL client, find another one who can. Death always blows open closet doors. It is an inevitable necessity to be at least selectively out to a trusted friend, a close family member, and to your lawyer. If you have joint banking accounts, make sure they are in order, to protect your money. If you own property, then make sure you know where the deed to the house is, and where all of the other important papers are kept. That is your security and will stand up in any court. Don't be a fool! Know that life is not guaranteed and at any moment you could be killed in a totally unpredictable accident, tornado, house fire, or other natural disaster. Don't wait until tomorrow, do it today.

Duane and I have a joint checking account. I am the beneficiary of his life insurance policy, and he is on mine. We both have wills that spell out what we want, and that he is to be included in every aspect of any final arrangements. We have told family members that if anything happens, they are to lean on the survivor of the relationship for advice. Let there be no doubt, there will not be any drama going on when our time is up. We suggest that you seek legal assistance to develop a will, or to get your affairs in order. There are web sites that can point you in the right direction.

Chapter 6

GOING BEYOND SIX MONTHS
"MAKE IT LAST FOREVER"

*If you are building a house and a nail breaks,
do you stop building or do you change the nail?*

~Rwanda proverb

Most of the brothers we know average six months of high interest in a man, then they start to get bored and move on to the next brother. Why is that? What is lost during those six months that make us throw in the towel, walk away, and never look back? How can you be in love with a brother; give him your all, e-mail him constantly, send him cards, give him gifts, and serve him wild and passionate sex for 6 months, one year, two years: and then with the blink of an eye, become bored. And how uncaring --- sometimes not even wanting to accept a dinner date at your favorite cafe anymore. What happens that turns everything sour? What is lost?

With many, it's because of getting caught up in the lust and not love. Many brothers fall in lust and rush into a relationship to get with the great sex, stunning good looks, or the money and connections our current object of desire has, ---everything but the inner man. It is easy to rush into the relationship for all the wrong reasons. It's easy to confuse infatuation with love. During the infatuation stage, we have time to see only what's on the surface, and any faults we may peep we overlook. Sometimes we rush because we are lonely, bored, or are struggling with low self esteem. We look at guys our age, think they are with lovers or think all our friends are in love, so we want to be in love too. Everything is for love. I have to laugh because I swore up and down about a million times that my previous lover was the one for life: That I was through with the games, clubs, and BS. No more drama for me. I had met my soul mate and we were going to buy that house, two cars, have a joint-checking account and have a cocker spaniel in the back yard. I was in love with being in love. I was caught up with Cupid.

I would like to share these steps that can give you a lifetime relationship with that one special brother.

1. It is possible to maintain a long-lasting relationship when it starts with a good friendship.

2. Don't have sex on the first date.

3. Avoid moving in for the first six months. He may be fine, but he looks even better when he has a place of his own.

4. Take time for yourself during the dating process. Give

him his space and you keep your space. It seems cliché, but absence does make the heart grow fonder. .

5. Do not under any circumstance neglect your friends just because you are getting to know him. Don't throw your friends away.

6. Never be afraid to reveal your true likes and dislikes during this maturation period. He can't be held responsible for that which he had no prior knowledge.

7. Always respect yourself and your partner..

8. Always encourage and support each other. .

9. Always say "I love you," even when you don't feel like it, but when your lover does need to feel it.

10. ALWAYS PROTECT YOURSELF.

A LOVE OF A LIFETIME

Mike and Phil's urban romance started out a few months before the 1967 Detroit riots; amidst the turmoil, turbulence and revolution of the Black Power Movement.

During a Detroit Easter Sunday religious service, Michael Petross and Phillip Pugh exchanged friendly introductions at a local church. That fine day marked the time both Petross and Pugh planted the seeds of a love that has become as strong a force as the Civil Rights and Black Power Movements. They created a love that has endured many trials and tribulations. Yet it still remains an example of just what two men can do when they are traveling on one accord.

"It was such a colorful and wonderful time with all those things going on...we were both active in learning about Black Culture, our sexuality and spirituality and we happened to attend the same church group," says Petross, a 56-year-old civil servant. "But, it wasn't until four years after we initially met that we started dating. And we have been together ever since."

Petross and his partner Pugh attribute their longevity to having mutual respect for one another and for being able to communicate frankly individual needs.

"We have been able to last for more than 33 years because we always talked things out and we were both able to not let jealousy get the best of our relationship," says Mike's partner Phillip Pugh, 60, who is presently retired and spends his days helping raise his two small, great-grand children along with Mike. Although it is difficult to accurately report just how many Black SGL male and/or Black lesbian households exist in America, many social scientists agree there are more than what many people choose to believe.

"There exists a prevailing myth in the Black gay and lesbian community, and in many cases in the majority mainstream and gay communities; that a relationship with two men or two women can't last or won't work... Because of a number of factors that include a misperceived notion of gay sexuality," says Baltimore counselor Henry Westray, LCSW.

"That old notion couldn't be further from the truth because there have been successful Black gay unions since the beginning of time. We just hear about all the negative ones." Westray says the success rate for any gay and/or lesbian relationship is rooted in how each individual couple chooses to work through such key

issues as:

1. Each partner's comfort level with his or her own sexuality.

2. How willing couples are to communicate their needs, desires and frustrations.

3. How effective couples are at establishing important ground rules for their union.

4. How openly gay each partner is going to be in both their personal and professional lives.

5. Whether the couple will be strictly monogamous, or whether other sexual boundaries can be successfully negotiated and maintained.

6. Whether the couple can maintain financial responsibility and share household chores.

Mike and Phil agree with Westray and say their relationship has been able to weather the storms (of what it means to be both Black and gay in America) because of one special ingredient: our commitment to each other.

"We had a burning desire to make it work," says Phil. "And we never tried to change the other person or control the other. I learned very early on that harboring feelings of jealousy was unhealthy for me. Why should I be bothered that someone would find Mike attractive when I, too, find him to be a charismatic and smooth, good-looking man and vice-versa. We established clear boundaries of just what will and won't take place with an outsider in our relationship. Our first commitment is to each other."

For Mick Daniels and Jeffery Wright in Seattle, openness is the key. "I tell Mick not to hold anything back. If he sees someone that looks good to him," says Jeffery. "I don't want him to act like he didn't or feel that he can't comment about what he sees or saw. That is too much stress, and I am confident in my relationship. I've told my partner, that if you find another brother that you just have to have, tell me about it, and let's do it together, or at least let me watch. I am a realist; I know if a man wants something badly enough, he is going to get it. So, I might as well accept that as the gospel, and give him the ok that

I want him to have whatever he wants. If it is another dick, then lets get it, take care of that desire, and go on with our relationship."

Jeffery's partner, Mick respects this kind of arrangement. "I've learned from many relationships that you cannot control another man. **(See chapter 3 on Free Will.)** So you might as well deal with it: and pray that when that time comes, you can deal with it together. Why give up a good relationship for five-minutes of pleasure?"

Dr. Mike Jackson, who specializes in counseling SGL relationships, shared his opinion about SGL relationships for this chapter:

"When two men start the dating process it can be very difficult. It is also during that period that both of you are putting your best foot and face forward. From day one if you want to be serious about a person, then you set a standard for him to follow. People will treat you how you allow. If you fall for everything he gives you in the beginning, you will crash and burn in the end. The courtship ritual can and should continue beyond the six-month period. Invest in the courtship ritual. Remember the first six months are only a transitory period toward what will be in your new relationship, and should be evaluated carefully.

Chapter 7

LIVING UNDER THE SAME ROOF

"MAKING A HOUSE A HOME"

A partner in the business will not put an obstacle to it. ~Ethiopian proverb

Moving in with another man is a huge step, especially if you are independent and set in your ways. You may like your clothes hung in a certain manner, like your kitchen arranged in a specific way. Somebody else may be messy and not have a problem with it. Needless to say it can be quite an adjustment to live with another man who has his own set of habits and idiosyncrasies.

The key to making it work is constant communication, compromise, and commitment. Before you even start looking for an apartment or house, you need to take time out to talk about your individual lifestyle habits. It may be helpful to test the waters by spending several weekends together at one another's apartments before you take the plunge and sign a joint apartment lease. Be yourself during those weekends. Do not change because you want to hide something you do or don't want him to see. If you pee with the toilet seat down and don't wipe it off, then continue to do just that. If you leave your dirty clothes on the floor, do exactly that. If you hate to wash the dishes and leave them in the sink, in hopes that someone else will wash them for you later like your big sister used to do, then leave them there. Whatever you do when you are at home, let your lover see it. Bring it all out and in the open so he knows up front what he's getting into. Be open to his criticisms. Do not get an attitude if he tells you that your home lifestyle drives him crazy. Be open to making changes, but at the same time stay true to yourself. Old ways and habits die hard.

What we decided to do before we moved in with each other was to spend time together at each other's places. James is the neat freak. He likes his things in order and properly put away. While I like to drop my clothes in the middle of the floor when I come home. It may have driven him crazy at first, but I was willing to change, if he could be patient. We sat down and talked about everything from A to Z. We also asked questions and shared our concerns for and about things we did to each other that rubbed us the wrong way. We made a promise to work out our quirks, rather than let them come between us.

The next major step is deciding where you will live. Will you live with him or vice versa? Will you give up both your apartments and move into a new place? If either of you is a homeowner then the decision is going to require some serious discussion on what the best move is for both of you. For this guide, we are going to assume both of you are in rental apartments and not condominiums.

What kind of space will work for both of you is the big question to decide. If you are not out to your family and friends, then a two or three bedroom is a must. A bed in at least two rooms can camouflage the fact that you are really sleeping with your "cousin" or "roommate" to the folks and friends that may come by to visit sometimes. Next is sitting down to talk about what appliances, furniture and other items you both are planning to bring to the new place. Plan on what goes into storage and what goes out to the garage sale. Does he want to get a dog? Would you get tired of hearing his parrot? Does he want to sleep with the window open and the radio on all night? We recommend that you make this a collaborative effort to make your new place a home.

NOW IS THE TIME TO TALK MONEY.

You both need to discuss your debts, credit status, income, monthly expenses and cash flow. This conversation is critical to the success of your relationship. If money is not right, then there is not enough love, sex, dinner waiting on the table when you come home, or anything else to make it work. Trust us on this one. Most divorces and separations are over unresolved money issues. Remember Gwen Guthrie's song, "Ain't Nothing Going On But The Rent?" She sang there is "no romance without finance." That's a true statement. We believe in an equal split when it comes to household expenses. 50/50 right down the middle is the policy in our home. Even if one of us makes more than the other makes, there is still an equal sharing of expenses. Be careful here, though, because when there is a great difference in income this alone can cause resentment, unless there is very clear communication of feelings. That is why it is important to have a conversation about credit, income, bills and debt when you start dating, especially before you move in with your partner. If not, it can cause some major problems in your relationship. The number one reason that couples (str8 and SGL) split up is because of money problems. Try to make love when your telephone is ringing off the hook from bill collectors. Try to knock boots when the landlord is knocking on your door saying the rent is past due. Try to make love when the electric company, not you, is about to turn off the lights, or when there is nothing to eat in the fridge but ice cubes. Not a pretty picture.

DOLLARS AND COMMON SENSE SUGGESTIONS:

1. Always keep a little rainy day fund tucked away somewhere.   A savings account or certificate of deposit will work. An emergency fund to cover basic expenses for eight months is the ideal plan.

2. Don't ever become so broke that you have to depend on your partner to support you. Get out of debt.

3. Pay bills on time and in full. Always have your own money.

4. Do not lend money. Do not borrow money. The preferred policy is my money is your money and vice versa. Freely give money as a gift. With appreciation, accept money as a gift: with a clearly spoken or written understanding that no repayment is expected.

5. Do not try to buy affection. That is a good way to squander money and to lose your partner's respect. Helping your partner get and keep a full or part-time job helps him develop self-respect.

6. Do not over-react to financial problems early in the relationship. View them as learning opportunities. Be truthful about what you have now, then plan and invest for the future.

7. Watch for signs of financial irresponsibility in your partner. Pay attention to procrastination in writing out a weekly or monthly budget. Unpaid loans to friends and credit denials are red flags. Discuss your short and long-term goals with your partner. Almost everything you do together will cost money.

8. Explore values with your partner, focusing on what you expect money to provide – basic utility, comfort, prestige, self-actualization or something else.

9. Consider a prenuptial agreement, if either partner has accumulated assets (i.e., real estate, commercial business or not-for-profit organizations) prior to the start of the live-in relationship.

10. Create a workable financial structure, dealing with such issues as who will pay bills, balance the checkbook, and research large purchases. Draw up a budget and decide who should pay which items. Those who fail to plan should plan to fail.

11. Consider a "yours, mine and ours" system of both separate and joint accounts.

12. Maintain credit in both partners' names.

Once you've established some strong financial ground rules, you can move on to creating a positive home atmosphere.

Here are our 10 Golden Rules to maintaining a happy home. They have worked well for us over the years:

1. Keep God first in your heart and home.

2. Never let negative energy and people into your home.

3. Respect each other's space.

4. Love each other and tell each other daily.

5. Don't use your home as a party spot, sex party location, or hang out spot for your single friends.

6. Never go to bed angry and upset with each other.

7. Pay all your bills on time.

8. Live within the ground rules of your relationship, while keeping everything in perspective.

9. Clean up after yourself.

10. Never use the words "my place" when discussing your home with friends, it's "our place"!

FAMILY, FRIENDS AND YOUR RELATIONSHIP

Having family and lots of friends is a wonderful thing. Nothing beats the joy and love we get from our loved ones. Their presence in our lives adds to our quality of life when they accept us for who we are and love us unconditionally. It's not about the quantity of friends you have, but rather the quality of those relationships that count.

Neither of us comes from a large family, so we have become family, in addition to being best friends. We have tried to expand our friendship circles, however we can never find brothers who vibe like we do. Many of the people we meet are single brothers who don't like to be around us because we are happy and in love. We have met some brothers we simply don't trust. We know that if given the opportunity, they would disrespect both of us, and try to have each of us sexually together or separately. That is not good karma to bring into the home. There are haters out there who would love to see us break up. We know to stay on high alert for home wreckers. When you are in a relationship you have to decide how you are going to deal with your friends, his friends, your family, his family. A serious thing to consider is how much you want everyone to know about your sexuality and the extent of your relationship with your partner.

We figured we would tell our family and friends more about our relationship after we established a stronger foundation and had been together for more than six months. When the time came for Duane and I to meet each other's family we were both nervous. I met Duane's family during a Thanksgiving dinner. We were a little scared. My anxiety caused me to sweat. Duane wanted to get his Grandmother's blessing first because of her special place in the family's life.

It went down like this.

IT'S A FAMILY AFFAIR.

Duane suggested we host a Thanksgiving dinner at our place. I was hesitant to support this decision, but because I knew this would be important to him, I agreed to the deal and gave him my support. This was the first time I would meet his family. Our relationship would be out when they came to the house. Since we lived in a one-bedroom apartment, we could not hide the fact that we slept together thanks to an open loft floor plan. We planned out a menu and chose to use a combination of catered dishes to complement a few things we cooked. Of course on the big day the dinner was a hot mess. The caterer called at the last minute to say their fryer was broken, that they couldn't delliver the fried turkey, and the macaroni and cheese was overcooked. In the meantime, his family was getting ready to come for dinner and we didn't have a complete meal to serve them. We quickly regrouped and asked his grandmother and aunts to bring some food. We also went out and bought a fresh turkey and opened a few cans of corn, cranberry sauce and veggies. I even whipped up my famous macaroni and cheese as we proceeded to save the meal. When his family arrived we were ready.

We had reserved the building's party room and decorated it with nice table settings as holiday music played in the background. It was going to be a good day after all. When the family arrived they rolled deep. There was his grandmother, the matriarch of the family, two of his five aunts and their children, plus a few cousins and his "closeted uncle". (Note: Duane and I knew he was gay, but he was keeping that on the low) Their warmth and down-to-earth personalities immediately made me comfortable.

After dinner we retreated to our loft for drinks, dessert and conversation. They wanted to get to know me, and I was anxious to check them out. It was a wonderful evening. We talked and laughed as family members told old childhood stories about Duane: those sentimental tales about his big head and runny nose. I learned a lot about Duane's upbringing from their visit. Duane's female cousins toured the loft and screamed over the garden-styled soaking tub in the spacious master bedroom, taking pictures as they sat around the porcelain bath. They were excited about the place being located so near the heart of the metropolis, with every convenience of urban living within walking distance. Being from a small town, they got a kick out of looking out the windows to see huge skyscrapers. The visit inspired a few of the female cousins to continue their education in order to leave the trap of the small town they lived in.

After a rocky start, our first Thanksgiving was a success and we were thrilled we made the decision to have the family over. They reacted to becoming fully aware of our SGL relationship basically by shrugging their shoulders and agreeing with cousin Phyllis who said, "Oh yeah, we knew all the time."

Duane had always wanted to host a Thanksgiving dinner at home with his partner, but in past relationships, previous partners were not supportive of the idea. I changed that and made his dream come true. This unselfish act made me realize that what we had in each other is truly very special.

Chapter 8

IS IT STILL GOOD TO YOU?
"HOW TO KEEP THAT LOVE FIRE BURNING"

Endurance pierces marble.

~Moroccan proverb

It is perfectly normal for the newness to wear off a relationship. Here's how to add a little kick to your romance:

1. Send flowers to his home if he lives alone. Brothers love to get flowers and if they don't it's because no one has ever sent them any. The biggest most masculine brother will be touched by this thoughtful gesture. If either of you is on the DL: sign the card with your initials. This will decrease those rumors that he's gay.

2. Create a spa environment in your home bathroom. Run him a hot bath, put scented candles around the tub, burn some oils and play a nice mellow CD of your partner's favorite music. Let him soak without any interruptions. Turn off his cell, pager and home phone and leave him alone and just let him get centered deep in thought. Later, after you dry off every inch of his body, massage him with hot oil.

3. Dress sexy. I personally like to surprise my man by not having any underwear on. I know some of you might say that is tacky, but it turns my bro out. He has a hard

time keeping his hands off my trouser snake when we are in private. So, it's on!

4. Find out what's his ultimate sexual fantasy, then fulfill it. Note: Be prepared if it does not include only you. Some men fantasize about having sex with other people. Your partner may want to add some male or female company to your bedroom. Speak up if you can't handle this. We know you are tripping on this one. But many men do like variety. I'd rather give my partner a 3-way sexual experience that includes me, than to have him seek out one I do not know about. Just be careful about who you bring home.

5. Wake him up with sex. Instead of reaching over to turn off the alarm clock, reach over and grab something else. There is nothing like early morning sex to start the day off with a big bang.

6. Cater dinner for two at home. I love to set the table for two with candles, some chilled wine, our favorite CD playing softly and a catering company doing all the work in the kitchen for my partner and me. While they

are slaving away in the hot kitchen, we are in another location in the house, getting our freak on. When we go into the dining room, everything is on the table ready and waiting to enjoy. Life can be wonderful at times like this.

7. Buy two round trip tickets for a surprise getaway weekend. Who doesn't love to just get away after a long stressful week? If you can't afford to fly, pack the car and head to your local state park. Rent a cabin and make love in the woods all weekend.

8. Give him a tastefully nude picture of you. Have it done professionally, that way he can see you in a birthday suit, even when you are out of town.

9. Make a home movie of the two of you making love. This could be a fun and exciting experience. It could just be an Oscar-winning performance. Note: we highly suggest that you destroy the video after you are finished watching it a couple times.

10. Hire a masseur for both of you. Get a brother to come to your place and let him rub the tension and stress

away. Sex afterwards is hot, hot, hot!

Other successful suggestions:

*Say, "I love you" everyday to each other.
*Tell your partner that he is sexy and fine, even when he is not feeling like he is. Compliments will get you everything and everywhere.

*Take your man out on a date. Just because you have been together for a few months or years doesn't mean you stop dating.

*Take him out like it was the first time you met him.
*Always be in "chase mode". What this means is never get too comfortable with your relationship and start taking it for granted.

*Always express how you feel about your man.
*Role-play. E-mail him at work and tell him that when he gets home, the plumber man will be there to lay some pipe. When he gets home, have on your utility shirt (which can be purchased at any thrift shop) and tell him you have an appointment to get busy, and you don't

know where to begin. During the conversation, get an erection, and make sure he sees the print. Then ask him to show you if work is needed, on the kitchen floor, in front of the sink....

Chapter 9

AGE IS NOTHING BUT
A NUMBER
"APRIL – OCTOBER RELATIONSHIPS"

If you intention is pure you can walk on the sea.

~Swahili proverb

The SGL community places a high premium on youth, the gifted and talented. Take a look at any of the popular web sites most of the ads clearly state a demand for those under 40, 30 or 25. To some brothers if you are more than 25 you are over-the-hill and if you are thirty-something you're practically a senior citizen who drinks Metamucil and dates Ben Gay. And please, Lawdy Miss Clawdy, don't be over 40! They'll think you have one foot in the grave already. That may not be right, and it may be immaturity talking, but it is a reality. Brothers peep this: in life you have three guarantees; One: you are going to pay taxes. Two: you are going to die. And three: if God blesses you long enough, you are going to get old. There are no ifs, ands or buts about that. There are some fine, well-built brothers 40+ who can run circles around brothers half their ages – giving up body for days, winning a game that's tight and strong and they have the sexual stamina to break a brother off in the bedroom.

Added maturity only age and experience can bestow upon a man, helps to establish clear boundaries as these men know exactly what they will or will not tolerate. This cuts down on potential drama, head games and lies. There's an old adage that says the blind can't lead the blind. When it comes to dating a more-mature brother, someone younger may find his experience a good teacher in this ever-changing world. However you have to be open and receptive to get beyond the age issue, to a place where you can appreciate a total package. It takes a discerning eye to see the value in what many older men bring to the table: higher income potentials, stability, an established professional life, a comfortable home and the confidence that comes from being a fully self-possessed man.

We asked our 30-year-old friend Gerald Washington if he would ever hook up with an older brother who really loved him and who was about 15 or 20 years older than he. "I don't want no man that's got more gray hair on his balls than on top of his head" says Gerald. "When I roll over in the morning I want to be inspired, baby, not reaching for a walker or cane." As a member of the 40+ club, our friend Eddie Kincaid disagrees. "I speak from what I know, an older man usually has reached a point in his life where he appreciates more than a quick fix and a six-pack," he told us. "We want culture, class, good conversation, goals, and a lifestyle that is real. Not one that is based on going to the gym just because you are trying to get into another sheer, sleeveless shirt to stand out at the club with all the other wannabes. Many times they have to go back to their mama's house, after the party is over." Over 40 is not old. Stop saying that it is. A person's outlook on life determines age, and you are only as old as you feel.

Conversely, there are occasions when a more mature man craves the company of a younger dude. Now that I've been 40-something for a while, sometimes I can relate to this. Once in a blue moon, I've found myself attracted to younger men, with whom I've shared memories of many good dates. Right now I'm nearly 18 years older than Duane and the age difference has not hindered us from enjoying each other. In fact I may never have considered hooking up with Duane if my prior positive experiences with younger men didn't encourage me. I remember the first time I dated a man 14 years my junior. Here is my story of a young love.

I met 21 year-old Byron Mays at a shopping mall. He was one of the sales associates at one of my favorite clothing stores. While he waited on me we found ourselves making a connection that went beyond a standard sales transaction. He was short, slim, energetic and full of life. Byron had waves in his hair, thick bushy eyebrows, a thick black moustache above luscious lips and a dimple in each cheek. He was just as cute as can be. I made a point to buy a few more items than I previously planned on once I found out he worked on commission. In exchange for my kindness, he inquired if I had a few minutes to spare and offered to buy me a root beer during his lunch break. I didn't have anything to do, so I figured why not. Byron's pretty boy looks had me mesmerized, yet I found myself a bit apprehensive about how far I should take our flirting because I knew I was at least a decade older than he. His sharp sense of humor was infectious and as we talked during his break I learned he had plans to pursue a career within the music industry. When I discovered he had not been to college I offered some fatherly advice and encouraged him to give college a try, considering how volatile the entertainment industry can be. He told me he really wasn't the college type. He was adamant about going to New York City to jump-start his career. A product of the BET and MTV video generation, he wanted a "bling-bling" lifestyle: full of cash, luxury cars and designer clothes.

We exchanged numbers and I promised him I'd call him to send more business his way. Later that evening he called me, and asked if I could give him a ride home. He had missed the bus and needed to get home to care for his grandmother. I agreed and picked him up in the mall's parking lot. On the way home, we talked and laughed about his customers and other events that happened at the store. When I got him home, he teased me about my age. "You are cool, for an old dude," said Byron. I could have slapped him. I wasn't all that old. Quick to come back—I said, "This old man could teach you a few things, son" as we both broke out in laughter. "Don't let my youth fool you, I may just teach you a few things," he said as he broke a sly smile and winked on the way out of the car. Byron's wink stayed with me for the rest of the ride home, following me into the house and into my dreams.

The next day he called me from work and asked if he could come over and chill out with me after he got off. I hesitated for a few seconds, then agreed to let him come over. He arrived early in the evening. When I opened the door he winked at me and had a dimple and a warm smile on his face. Byron walked into my place like he'd been there a thousand times before. He liked my sense of décor and told me my crib was phat. "I could see myself chillin' in a place like this one day," said Byron. I offered him some bing cherries to snack on, and we sat in front of the TV watching the news, also eating a few sandwiches and talking about the day. The conversation was lightweight until he hit me with something I didn't expect. "Do you mess around?" he asked just as plain as day. I almost fell off the couch as I tried to maintain my composure, wanting to know further what he meant. "Don't play stupid. Do you mess around with men, or with guys?" He was blunt and bold with what he had to say while his eyes pierced into mine without a blink or twitch. He was looking straight in my face and all I could say was, "Why?" "Did I do something to make you ask that question?" I asked. "No. But I know you are into me. I can tell by the way you look at me," said Byron. "Plus, you haven't said a word about a girlfriend, or your woman.

You know the usual conversation brothers have when they are fucking a woman." His bold honesty was appealing. I had no choice but to inquire. I asked, "Are you in the life, or kick it with dudes? I do." "Yep, I knew it. Let's fuck around! I like you and I want to see you totally naked," he said – explaining that he'd never before gone all the way with a guy, only jacking off with a cousin and giving his best friend head during a sleep-over visit. He wanted to know what it felt like to go all the way with a man.

"Byron, I'm too old for you," I said. "What does age have to do with anything?" he said "Plus you look young and don't look or act your age. How old are you anyway?" I never revealed my age to him. We ended up in my bedroom and I turned him out, by turning him on to frottage.

Over the next year, our sexual trysts developed into a full-blown romance. I was his first male lover and he brought a much-needed dose of enthusiasm back into my life because of his youthful optimism. He valued how he could explore his sexuality with me. I must admit we had a few adjustments to make.

Although I enjoyed our sex life, there were times when I felt pressured to keep up with his high sex drive. There would also be times I'd become resentful when he couldn't relate to some of the professional battles I was fighting in the workplace. Although he had heard about racism and discrimination, he could not fully comprehend the impact the notorious corporate glass ceiling had on my spirit. On his end, he found my homebody ways nerve-racking. Because we were at two different income levels, he would get frustrated that he didn't have the number of material possessions I had. These differences caused a rift in our relationship that was further widened by our individual goals. He wanted more than anything to move to New York, and I just didn't see myself with him there. I knew better than to try to convince him that he should stay in Memphis. So, it didn't surprise me at all when he came by one day and said he was moving to the Big Apple to live with an aunt.   Before he left, he told me he'd never forget the time we spent together, and that he'd always utilize the life lessons I taught him. I wished him the best and offered to drive him to the bus station when he was ready to leave. That day, just before boarding that northbound Greyhound, Byron broke that sly smile and winked at me. He was confident, cocky and ready to take on the world.

I had learned something powerful: love transcends age. Although love transcends age, we do not condone dating people who are under-age. However, when it comes to consenting adults in private, that's another matter.

Chapter 10

WHAT IFS
"SCANDALOUS SITUATIONS AND SCENARIOS"

There are three things that if a man does not know, he cannot live long in this world: what is too much for him, what is too little for him and what is just right for him.

~Swahili proverb

UNFORTUNATELY, THINGS FELL APART.

Dennis met Steve in the lobby of the theater at intermission, struck up a conversation, and agreed to continue their conversation when the final act was over. After an in-depth discussion of the play over several cups of gourmet coffee, they exchanged numbers and met up later that week. They both wanted to believe it was love at first sight. They were both lonely, wishing for a dream lover. Within weeks they were talking about moving in together. Setting up house. They were in love. They spent every minute together. Dinners, and long walks in the park, they would have breakfast together every Saturday. Dennis thought they had it going on, sending cards and flowers to each other. It was nothing for them to buy each other jewelry and clothes-- just because. Steve said, "it was probably less than three weeks after Dennis moved in that we had picked up the application to open up a joint checking account, and were planning a trip together to Montreal for the holidays." They had decided to move in together as soon as one of their leases had expired, and they did. It was heaven. Dennis said that he would tell his friends, that God does work miracles, giving God the praise for this (unforeseen, unplanned) mess while things were going smoothly. If only he knew what he was getting into.

Then it happened. One day, they got into an argument about Dennis leaving his dirty clothes on the floor when he undressed. He said "Steve that is a bad habit that I have, and I am working on it." He had picked up after himself most of the time, because he knew that his new love was a neat freak. But, this day he just didn't feel like taking the clothes to the laundry room, and left everything on the floor. When his lover, came into the room, he just went off on him, went ballistic, acted out, performed as if he was up for an Oscar. Steve told Dennis, "you have not mopped the floor in the kitchen, as you said you would, you left dirty dishes in the sink, you left clothes all over the floor in the bedroom, you didn't clean out the shower, and you didn't even take out the trash. I'm tired of picking up after your sorry lazy butt!" "And if you want a maid," Steve said, raising his voice and pointing his finger, "you need to take your trifling butt home to your mama's house, and let her pick up behind your sorry late butt".

Dennis, who is nobody's punk, told Steve " you can kiss my late, trifling, sorry, lazy butt and go straight to hell! I'm tired of hearing you nag, nag, nag, nag, nag, nag, nag!" From that comment, the argument escalated into a fist swinging "back alley" kind of fight. Knocking over lamps, overturning furniture, kicking, biting, pulling, and cussing. The only thing that saved them from themselves was that the neighbor knocked on the door because she heard the noise and commotion. When it was all over, Steve did not look up at Dennis. He just sat there in a daze, staring straight ahead. Both of them were all beat up. Both were a bloody mess. Dennis wanted to say more to him, wanted to apologize, but his pride wouldn't let him. He just turned and walked out of the house. Walked out of his home; a place that he had loved coming home to. He felt like a fool. How could he have let it get to this point? Why must he now start over again? Dennis was hurt and feeling about half past dead. They had loved each other. If only they had taken time to get to know each other, then maybe things would have worked out better. Dennis got into his sleek silver Saturn Ion and drove away with a heavy heart.

Steve opened the door and assured his neighbor everything was fine and that she shouldn't call the police. That comment showed Steve to be a liar and a fool. Domestic violence is real. To lie about it is the wrong response to it. For adults to allow their private lives to become public is foolish. We'll take a second closer look at domestic violence in a later chapter. For now consider that Steve and Dennis went from being in love, to being in hate because they didn't take the time to become friends first. They didn't have a foundation that would help them deal with problems that can arise in relationships. You may find yourself in a few predicaments from time to time. To help prepare you for those rough days, we have created a series of potential situations that may test your ability to communicate with your partner, your ability to think before you react to your partner, and your willingness to maintain a level head and demonstrate adult maturity and restraint. We encourage you to take time out to decide how you would handle these scandalous scenarios by indicating how you might respond to each vignette. (Our recommendations are listed also). Be honest with yourself as you have fun with these. Hopefully you will get a new feel for how you can respond to the unexpected.

GUESS WHO'S COMING TO DINNER?

What if you come home early one day and find a built and buffed good-looking sexy brother watching television with your partner? You don't know this man from Adam.

Do you:

A. Start acting like a fool, cussing your partner out and accusing him of cheating on you.

B. Come in, introduce yourself to the stranger in a nice and cordial way and ask your partner to go with you to another room where you ask him who this person is.

C. Come in, sit down with them, roll your eyes at your partner and give him major attitude until the guest gets up and leaves.

Our answer: B Why act like a fool? This could be a co-worker of your partner's, a relative or even an old friend from his high school you have not met because he's from out of town. If you react in a negative way it could back fire and cause a breakdown of trust in your relationship. You don't own your partner (remember free will?). He's a grown man, and is with you because he wants to be.

MR. TELEPHONE MAN

What if you over hear your partner on the phone telling someone that he can't wait to see him or her later.

Do you:

A. Get an attitude as soon as he gets off the phone. When he asks you what is the problem you give him the silent treatment.

B. Pull the phone cord out of the wall, or drop his cell phone into the toilet, then proceed to cuss him out because you know he's cheating on you from what you just heard.

C. Give the man the privacy he deserves. When he hangs up, ask him in a neutral way who he had been talking to.

Our answer: C. If there is real trust in a relationship, you don't have to worry about anything. He could have been talking to his mother. If he knows you overheard him, he might tell you whom he was talking to. Do not over react.

FUNNY DISCOVERIES

What if you find condoms and a half-empty bottle of KY lube in your partner's gym bag that you know he didn't use with you?

Do you:

A. Confront him on why he has these items in his gym bag and wait to hear what he says.

B. Don't say anything about the rubbers, but tell him you want to go with him to the health club next time he goes.

C. Start packing your clothes because you know he's cheating on you and you don't want to know with whom: you have all the proof you need.

Our answer: A. Tell him you accidentally saw the condoms and lube in his bag, and you want to know why he has these items. Then you wait for his answer.

WHEN HE'S NOT WHERE HE SAID HE WOULD BE:

What if you see your partner out with another man you don't know? You are surprised to see him because he told you he was going to be at his parent's house, or working late.

Do you:

A. Run up to him, grab him, push him to the ground and start beating him down. Then do the same thing to the brother he is with.

B. Don't let him see you. Just walk away and when he gets home you have his stuff packed and on the steps outside.

C. Go up to him, speak in a friendly greeting and wait to see what he does next.

Our answer: C Go up to him and see if he sweats, has nothing to say, or gets a look on his face that says he knows he's busted. Or does he choose to introduce you to the brother, and ask you to join them for the rest of the day or evening?

WHEN THE THRILL IS GONE:

What if your desire for sex with your partner is gone? There is no longer a spark in your sex life.

Do you:

A. Talk to him about it and see if there is something you both can do to bring it back.

B. Get some trade on the side to satisfy your sexual needs.

C. Ask your partner if he would consider inviting a third person to join the two of you in bed.

Our answer: A (of course). In every relationship the passion and desire for the person you sleep with day in and day out will not be as strong as it was in the beginning. But you can do a number of things to bring back the spark (see chapter 8 **Is It Still Good To You**). We know what to do when we need a shot of passion. It comes from being in tune with our sexual fantasies and desires. Do not get too cocky and think that your hot rod is made of gold. There are hundreds of other bigger, thicker, and harder pieces out there just waiting for your partner.

GONE TOO LONG:

What if your partner stays out all night long and comes home in the morning and doesn't say anything about where he's been?

Do you:

A. Change the door locks so he can't get in.

B. Wait up all night, calling his cell phone and all his friends, family and the police because you are worried.

126

When he finally comes home, you let him in, and let him know how worried you've been and that you're glad to see that he is safe.

C. Have breakfast waiting on him when he comes home, give him some love, and go on about your day. Then you stay out the next night.

Our answer: B Anyone who'd stay out all night and not call needs to have his butt whipped—figuratively speaking, of course. It's unfair for him to make you worry. This behavior also should put you on high alert that he's creeping on you, or that he's doing drugs or something: especially if he can't prove where he was and why he did not call. If his attitude is such that he feels he does not have to check in and out about his movements and he says that what he does is his business, the relationship may need to be terminated.

HE WAS A FRIEND OF MINE:

What if you find out that your partner has been having sex with your best friend, or with his best friend?

Do you:

A. Confront them both about your finding and talk about it.

B. Call the other person, and cuss them out, and then cuss your partner out before you put him out of the house, or declare that you are leaving.

C. Get even. Have an affair of your own, or start sleeping with his best friend too.

Our answer: A. Find out what caused him to cheat on you. If you don't, this will affect your future relationships and self-esteem. It is good to find out what caused your partner to have an affair outside of your relationship. If it was for a reason you can forgive and you both do not want to end the relationship, then work it out together. We advise you to have the other person in on that conversation. If you can't forgive this transgression, move on.

FLIPPING THE SCRIPT:

What if your partner, who has only been a top or bottom in your relationship wants to flip and do the opposite?

Do you:

A. Freak out because you can't perform the way he wants,

even though you want to.

B. Try and give him what he thinks he wants from you.

C. Don't you do it. Tell him that's not your flavor, but you talk it out and see what can be done to satisfy his new desire.

Our answer: C. Sometimes a top will want to try sex in the bottom position to see what that feels like. Or a bottom will want to climb into the top position and release with some frottage. These feelings may arise and both of you will have to deal with them. Some of us may not be able to be penetrated like old-fashioned bottoms usually can with enjoyment. You are not less in love if you absolutely cannot stand the pain of the anal thing, and cannot receive your partner's erection. Caution: anal sex is the most risky HIV transmission route. See chapter 20 for details on the pleasures and enjoyment of frottage.

ROCKING AT THE SEX PARTIES:

What if your partner wants you to attend a sex party with him?

Do you:

A. Go with him for the fun of it and make sure he doesn't let anyone else have sex with him.

B. Agree that if you go, your partner has to deal with what might happen and how it might affect the relationship.

C. Both of you attend with the understanding that you can have sex with whomever you want. You agree to limits on what you can and can't do (i. e., kissing, sucking or whatever is off limits for the relationship's well-being).

Our answer: A. Why not go together? If your partner wants to attend a sex party, then why not go with him. Just make sure you talk about it before you get there and set some ground rules. You might have some fun, and not even have sex.

Steve and Ray, a Chicago couple interviewed for this book, actually met at a sex party. "As soon as we saw each other we hooked up, and ended up in a corner talking the entire night," says Steve. "We did do a little something later on that night after the sex party, but we were not a couple. We have talked about going to sex parties now that we are a couple and have decided that's not our thing. But the other guy has the right to attend one if he wants to."

130

Chapter 11

THE INTERNET AND YOUR RELATIONSHIP
"POINT & CLICK"

Small matters breed important ones.

~Ivory Coast proverb

The Internet is a valuable and important communication tool. It has made the world a smaller place and has allowed many of us to expand businesses and to find outlets for relaxation and information. The Internet also gives many brothers the opportunity to meet other brothers around the world. Some encounters develop into short-term relationships, while others lead to one-night stands. When it comes to the World Wide Web and your relationship, make sure you don't let it get between you and your partner. Activities that put your real-life relationship in danger include the following: Placing personal ads to meet other men will make your partner wonder why you are so eager to meet them. Spending too much time in chat rooms talking to other men will make your partner wonder why you choose strangers over him for conversation. Cruising sexually explicit sites for naked pictures of unusually well endowed brothers, with tight bubble butts, may leave your partner feeling inadequate, neglected or no longer the main attraction of your love life. Be sure to talk with your lover to reach an understanding of what is appropriate behavior for each of you. We know many people also may use chat rooms and other Internet features for research and networking opportunities. However when these modern electronic marvels are used for sexual stimulation, which does not include your partner, you are treading on thin ice. Particularly if your partner is sensitive, insecure or jealous his feelings can be hurt if he knows that most of your free time is spent sitting in front of the computer screen looking at dozens of men in their birthday suits. This may create unnecessary tension and create a lack of trust, as was the case with Harold Deveraux, a New Orleans based webmaster.

HAROLD'S E-MAIL NIGHTMARE:

Harold attempted to start an on line escort service and one of his responsibilities was to recruit men interested in becoming members within the pool of available escorts. While this was not a secret he tried to keep from his partner, he did not come out to fully disclose this plan ahead of time. He met Calvin, a brother chillin' in the park who expressed a willingness to work as an escort. The two exchanged e-mail addresses and phone numbers. Harold was eager to check out Calvin's sexual skills, given his screen name, Mr. Asp. Harold failed to tell his own

133

partner about the meeting. Two days later he followed-up with Calvin and sent an e-mail explaining how he enjoyed meeting Mr. Asp, and that he looked forward to getting him up again. In a hurry, Harold didn't properly log off his computer, and his partner got on the computer and read the message sent to Calvin. His lover became very pissed off over Harold's e-mail to Calvin. He did admit that curiosity got the best of him and he became nosey and checked Harold's e-mail, but Harold admits he was at fault. First he should have told his partner about the meeting. Although he exercised his free will to do whatever he wanted to do, no questions asked, it caused a rift in the relationship that took about six months to fully resolve.

If you are going to continue to look at personal ads and check the hottest Black male web sites, tell your partner. If you are going to visit the popular on-line chat rooms, then just make sure your partner knows you are continuing to be active online. If your partner feels uncomfortable about it, listen to his reasons. Further examine your own actions and articulate why you have a need to surf the web: is it for networking purposes, research, or are you getting aroused sexually from the experience. If you find that you're getting a sexual kick from logging onto various chat rooms your lover may view that as a form of infidelity and you must be aware of that. It does not matter that the person you chat with is 1547 miles away. It is about the emotional intimacy you may share with your faceless new friend that may cause a lover to see this as being unfaithful. A word to the wise for all who are making hookups on line.

INTERNET HOOKUPS BLAMED FOR RISE IN AIDS:
According to two new studies, presented at the 2003 National Prevention Conference, a growing number of same gender loving and bisexual men in the USA are engaging in risky sex with partners they meet on the internet. This is raising fears that the AIDS virus could be poised for a major comeback in the group hardest hit by the epidemic. Online chat rooms and web sites are replacing bathhouses and sex clubs as the most popular meeting points to arrange high-risk sex. However, a study in the December 2003 issue of the journal Sexually Transmitted Diseases shows that gay men who use the Internet to find sex partners are no more

likely to have unprotected anal sex than gay men who meet their partners in other venues. Earlier studies have connected gay men who use the Internet to find sex with a greater risk of sexually transmitted diseases, including HIV infection. But the study, conducted by researchers in Atlanta of more than 150 sexually active gay men, showed that incidences of unprotected anal sex, which carries the highest risk of HIV infection, were about the same among Internet and non-Internet users. The study did find that gay men using the Internet to meet sex partners had a higher but modest risk for other STDs. This is mostly because they also were shown to be more likely to engage in anal sex of all types, have group sex, have anonymous sex in bathhouses and sex clubs, and use recreational drugs. "Internet sex-seeking may not be associated with having unprotected anal sex or having relatively greater numbers of sex partners," the researchers concluded. "However, Internet sex-seeking gay men may have a modestly enhanced risk of STD acquisition and transmission."

At one point in time your lover was the coolest cat to you. Don't let your mouse run him out.

Chapter 12

SIZE DOES MATTER

"I'M PACKING TEN INCHES"

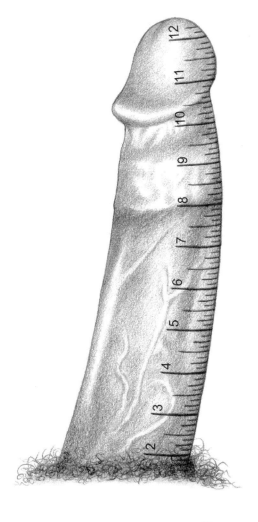

He who asks questions, Cannot avoid answers.

~Cameroon proverb

That BIG question, "Does size really matter?," has been asked by both men and women for years. I would not doubt that cave men asked their sexual partners this same question. It amazes me that some brothers put more emphasis on the size of their erection than on their education, job, health or their families. It seems that the American credo "the bigger the better" truly applies in the sexual arena. No matter what his race, creed or color, to have a large phallus is one of the most desired qualities of any man. Even heterosexual men inspect each other in the gym showers, in hope that they measure up. They may not desire to have and to hold the other man's phallus, but the extremely competitive nature of the US male overrides sexual orientation in the need to see how he compares. Those men, who have been blessed, to be especially well endowed will use that natural fact to make up for other qualities that they might be lacking. I know many men who are packing an average six-inch penis, but they will tell anyone who asks that they have at least four to five more inches. Not many of us are willing to be truthful about what we really have behind our zippers. Visit some of the popular web sites, you will find: Big Dick Brothers,

Horse Hung Black Studs, Big Black Bucks, and other descriptions that make it plain that if you ain't packin', you ain't welcome. Or, if you are packing, then come on in and join the big dick brotherhood.

The large size of his penis, or worse, the small size a man has to offer his partner can make or break relationships. When you are size-struck you have in mind a mandatory minimum size the brother you are interested in must have. You may think he's fine; that he has a great personality, that he lives in a lovely home, that he's in an interesting career, and that he's all that and a bag of chips. But when you are truly a "size queen," none of that matters as much as how much meat the man has between his legs.

When I have met brothers who sport a long, thick penis and they prefer to be a bottom, I think, "what a waste, all that beef, and he does not want to use it." I was involved with a brother several years ago, and he was a 100% bottom. The bro was packing a proven, ruler measured 10 and a half-inch erection. And this dude hated his penis. He had the natural lubricant smegma. That is the oily substance, often called "head cheese," which allows the foreskin to glide easily back and forth. Many SGL men share a strong fetish for foreskin, and uncut men are highly prized and sought after. He told me that he wished he had a smaller dick because it seemed to him that every time he met a potential partner he got stereotyped. When a potential partner saw that massive male member they figured all he would want to do is fuck with brute force 24/7. Or other potential partners want to focus all their attention on his hulking hard-on, and it becomes the ultimate sex object. No love, tenderness, sensitivity, or feeling of sensuality: just a frenzied response of excitable sexual submission. He shared with me that many times he had given in to being pressured to be the top: because the "so called" top he was with was so size struck. For some very well endowed brothers, what others may envy, they almost get bored with and tired of. Through history Black men have been objectified, feared and devalued. My partner Duane's last lover had the build of a pro football player, over six feet tall, 240 pounds but with a very small dick. Duane said, his ex was so little that on rock hard it was only four inches. But, he made up for having such a small one in other ways. Duane shared with me that it didn't bother him that his ex had a worm and not a snake. Duane says it's not the size that counts, it's the motion of the ocean. He thinks that guys should avoid anal penetration with large ones anyway, and extra large ones, especially. They could do some serious damage. These days and times SGL men should learn to value each other on a deeper level. And besides, what really bothered Duane was that his ex would always put himself down, and repeatedly apologize for what nature gave him.

A THIN LINE BETWEEN LOVE AND HATE.

Men have a love-hate relationship with our penises, or whatever you call yours: dick, jimmy, bird, tool, wang, pecker, prick, piece, pole, p-p, we-we, wiener, cock, love machine, little friend, my best buddy, hot rod, trouser snake, or it. Some men give theirs a name. We've met Mr. Asp, and other snake references are also quite popular, King Cobra, Black Mamba, and one unusually well endowed man named his Dr. Anaconda.

We love our penis when we are having sex, and making our partner scream and holler at the top of his lungs. Also we are proud when we are told: both by other men or women that we are huge.

We love our penis, when it gets hard and stays hard. We love our penis when it gives us pure satisfaction when we are alone. No other human needed. We love the conveniences of being able to stand up and pee, of being able to be aroused on a moment's notice, and of being able, sometimes furtively, sometimes boldly to entice a potential sexual partner by showing a revealing print in our pants.

We love our penis, the moment when a new sexual partner cannot conceal joy and delight to see or to feel that it is larger than expected. Or we meet a fine new potential partner, and everything is wonderful because he says he is thrilled that yours is bigger than his.

We love it when another SGL man can see (by chance or glance) that it is bigger than his. It is so satisfying when his longing gaze says, "wow, man, sure wish mine was as big, as thick, as long, or sporting as prominent a mushroom head as yours."

We love our penis when it creates such a tight bond in our lives, that our partner cannot get enough of it. When we control our little head with the brain in our thinking head, we also control and limit the potential for excessive drama in our lives.

As quiet as it's kept, we love it because we know that it is our ticket to male privilege in this sexist world. While we may from time to time want to trade it in for a bigger model, we know it will never go out of style like a used car. How many times have you said, "well, Mr. Tallawacker, you sure make me feel good first thing in the morning." I know I have said that more times then I can remember.

We all know it ain't easy being a penis! He has a head he can't think with, an eye he can't see out of, and he has to hang around with two nuts all the time. His closest neighbor is a butt hole. And worst of all, he knows that if his owner can't find a date on a Saturday night, he is going to get beat.

We can occasionally hate our penis. When it gets caught

in our zipper, we blame it, for being in the way. We can still remember when our sweet candy stick embarrassed us, because we got caught playing with it at an inappropriate time or place. Our penis can get us in trouble. An unwanted pregnancy, with its life-changing consequences, is the prime example.

We really hate our penis when it starts to itch, burn, or drip when we pee. When it forces us to go to the local clinic to find out what is wrong.

If you really take a look at your relationship with your penis, you will discover that most of the time you love it, but our sexually repressed society encourages you hate it.

I have had the opportunity to talk to over 500 men about their penis while working on this book. I have talked to professional men; doctors, teachers, firemen, police officers. I have talked to drug dealers, users, homeless men, ministers, accountants, ex prisoners on parole and off parole. I have talked to old, young, short, tall, dark, light, educated, uneducated and even a few deaf men about their penis.

There has been many a great man, knocked down and out because he let his penis get the best of his best judgement. Many stories are told of a famous man, who because of his need to satisfy lust, lost.

The worst way to misuse a penis is to knowingly have penetrative sex with one, which carries HIV, and fail to wrap it in a condom. In this case life, disease and possible premature death is in the penis.

Why don't we take better care of one of the most valued parts of our bodies? Most men couldn't tell you the basic internal structure of the male sex organ. Many don't know the ten parts that make up the reproductive system. Many don't know anything about the signs of testicular cancer. That is one of the most common types of cancer in men ages 15 to 34. How many men know how to perform a testicular self-examination? Most men put their hands on their penis at least 10 to 20 times per day, but couldn't tell you if there is anything that doesn't feel right with their penis. As long as it gets hard on demand, it is in perfect condition. Wrong.

Let me stop here and back up.

I think it starts back when we are little boys. We were never taught to feel good about our penis. We are told that if we play with it, we are nasty, that if we use it the wrong way, we will make babies. We are given scary, dire warnings to protect it from zippers, kicks, and glue.

We should be taught as boys that our penis is a gift from God, and we should be proud and happy with what the creator gave us. We were given this gift to make life, and to give pleasure to our partner, or spouse. We ought to be told by our elders, our grandfathers, fathers and the men who raised us that we should keep our penis healthy, and not allow it to be infected, or cause us mental stress. I wish someone had told me that my penis could get me in trouble, and that I needed to make sure that I always was in control, that I should never let my little head, over rule the head that has my brain in it. I never got that conversation.

Ready for me to answer the BIG question? Yeah, I'm sportin' more than four! LOL! No, I'm not packing nine or ten inches. Matter of fact to be fair I measure mine in the proper way, to get an even comparison. Some guys exaggerate by measuring from beneath the scrotum. The curvature of their balls sack adds two or three inches to the tape measure. To be fair, look down, and start from the base on the top-side of the your shaft, to the tip. Include the extra length of foreskin overhang. I frustrate those who didn't do their homework in high school math class, first by saying I've got 203 millimeters. That is to say my erection measures 20 point 3 centimeters. When they gripe and complain and demand a straight up English answer I finally stop beating around the bush and say. Oh, a little more than average. (LOL) Ok, Ok, Ok the answer is I'm five inches with a soft-on and overhanging foreskin and (drum roll) a nice thick juicy eight inch boner.

When I read that the average length of an erect penis is six inches, my prejudice kicked in. Man, I thought to myself, "they must have included a lot of Caucasian and Asian guys to come up with that figure. I've been with and seen more eight-plus inches on brothers than brothers with six or less."

My good friend Keith in Los Angeles shared this story with me. *Last night my roommate Glenn asked me if I wanted to be in a three-way with him. A couple of Glenn's Latino banjee boyz want to be in one, and when they found out Glenn had a roommate, they immediately asked if I was "cute". And if I was, then they were down for it. I'm really concerned for Glenn on this one because my wang is bigger than his wand. If those bottoms get me, they'll forget all about Glenn and will want to just hit it with me. Then there will be all kinds of drama and jealousy in the house, and I can do without all that. Besides, Glenn has a complex about his size. He only has about five inches on hard, but when I hear him in the bedroom getting down, his partners seem to really like him. Every bottom I end up getting with falls in love with my pinga, because I have a nice thickness, a dark brown shaft, a caramel complexion head, plenty of foreskin, and it curves to the left. I have been described as, "perfect," by virtually all the brothers who love to give head and Latino guys love a brother with a two-toned, artistically sculptured pinga."*

When I go back east I also check in with my Buckeye buddy Pete. He is one of those brothers who will only date or have sex with brothers who are well hung. He's kind of stuck-up actually. If their manhood is not as big, (thick or long) as his, he is not interested. He works for the police department in Cleveland, and has spent some time working in the intake department. He has shared with me how many (and I quote the term he used) huge monster dicks he has seen on arrested suspects when they have to strip down for processing. He once told me about this little brother, busted with three pounds of weed. He stood just 5'4" and weighed about 130 pounds and his piece was so big it must have put 15 pounds between his legs. Pete said that when the brother took off his boxer shorts, everybody in the room gasped at the size of that tube steak. Even the captain of the shift: his eyes popped out in astonishment. There is something extra impressive about a really big dick on a really little guy.

No doubt about it: neither shoe size nor hand size will correlate with dick size. Pills and vacuum pumps will lengthen your love machine only temporarily.

However, viagra and similar pills are readily available and are excellent for men with impotence. See your MD for a sample pack and more information. You are not alone, there are many men who suffer from problems with their penis. Go get help. It will change your life, and improve your self esteem.

Many couples will start cheating if they haven't developed enough of a love bonding intensity to minimize the importance of dick size. I was in a relationship about ten years ago with a brother who had a tiny little prick. Maybe if I hadn't experienced so many other guys before who were packing more inches and thickness then it wouldn't have been such an issue for me. But it did have an adverse impact on our sex life. Now giving him head was a breeze. I could take in his dick and balls, no problem, but cuddling and grinding left a lot to be desired (no pun intended). I kinda felt sorry for the guy. He could tell my attitude was almost that of having sex with him as a charitable gesture. The relationship ended because of this, and looking back, I was wrong for basing my feeling about him on his small penis size. I ignored all those good qualities about him that had attracted me to him in the first place. After all he is a spiritual being having a very human experience. What I did was to reduce him to a physical being, and gave him a very dispiriting experience.

The only advice that I can give on this issue is that love is more than just the size of a dick. A big dick won't make you happy when you are down and out and need a hug or a kind word to help you make it through. A big dick can't be at the hospital when you are sick, or be there for you when you need support for a project you are working on, or if your boss is on your back, and you want to quit. Love is more than about the size of an organ, unless that organ is your heart. That is the only organ in your body that you should listen to when it comes to love.

Chapter 13

No Fats, No Fems
"Masculine and attractive brothers only"

Beauty and pride go to the grave.

~Swahili proverb

Have you ever checked out what brothers want in other men when they are in search of a hook-up? In almost every Internet ad, erotic magazine personal ad and 1-(900) PHONE SEX HOTLINE YOU ARE SURE TO FIND THESE DEMANDS:

1. Be a thug, (or at least look like one) .

2. Be on the down low, (or at least act like you are) .

3. Be 100% masculine: Act like a real man. Dress like a real man. Walk, talk, and act like a real man.

4. Be physically fit. (A 33 inch waist or smaller is preferred) A six-pack doesn't hurt, and have pecs and biceps of steel.

5. Be "straight appearing" at all times, especially in public.

6. Be discreet with what you say and how you say it. Be totally non-clockable.

7. Have your own place.

8. Have a dick no less than 8 inches with the ability to maintain a firm erection all night long.

9. Be a top. Be a bottom. Be oral.

10. Be younger than 30 but if you are older be in shape and have a youthful attitude and appearance.

As you can see, it's all about the look and the degree of super-butch masculinity a man possesses. In this lifestyle many brothers log a lot of hours per week at the gym or working out in their homes. Gyms and health clubs have become hot spots for meeting men for sex, socializing and networking. Too many of us only work hard at working out in order to win one game: the game of best outward appearances. We can't wait until summertime to wear those tight outfits that reveal the hard pecs, brawny biceps and powerful thighs that attract men: (and women, to wrongfully abuse as DL mendacity covers). This hard core thug is King / you are weak if you're a Queen attitude not only is creating a separate society within the Black same gender loving community, but it also is creating serious issues of poor (down) low self-esteem. That, in the long run, will cause hurt to both the artificially esteemed homothug and pain to the put-down effeminate men. No doubt that these attitudes formed from the impact of the culture in American society. In this first decade of the 21st Century, America has become an empire with an enormous ability to influence and to impact upon the rest of the world in many ways. The dominant white Anglo-Saxon Protestant culture's media insists this is a benevolent Christian country. But first lets do a little miscellaneous free association consideration of various ideas:

America is sexist. Therefore effeminate men bear the brunt of the inequity in the treatment of people with feminine qualities. Although it seems, that the very worst of hatred is suffered by our brothers in Jamaica. Official indifference there by the Attorney-General, Director of Public Prosecutions and the Metropolitan Police Commissioner are allowing a wave of reggae hit songs to advocate the shooting and burning of people, called Chi Chi Men, who are perceived to be same gender loving. In Zimbabwe the rape of women perceived to be lesbian, by police, is an ongoing atrocity. For a nation's policy to be that a lesbian can become heterosexual if she is raped is yet to be effectively addressed by human rights advocates. In this first decade of the 21st Century about 25% of young African-American men have been in jail, on parole or probation. U. S. prisons confiscated so many belts from inmates that wearing blue jeans halfway off their butt became a commercially-sold fashion statement on the street.

156

The Pentagon's military-industrial complex has a vise-grip on the government. Just by asking, it was able to pick up an $87 billion dollar supplemental appropriation, in an era of budget cuts for others. Is it any wonder that a tough, defensive, brute-force posture passes for manliness? Don't ask, and don't tell!

Black men seem too caught up in a live real fast, die real young position in life, and "in the life". Youth rules the agenda of BET, MTV and FM radio. Commercial media, driven by the demand to boost bottom line quarterly profits will inherently have values which are short-term and superficial. It is easier to buy into what is broadcast passively than to challenge it actively to create change. The silent partner in these various cultural dynamics is AIDS. Called the "thin man's disease" in Africa, AIDS has taken out the entire generation born between 1950 and 1980 in several nations south of the Sahara. In image-conscious Black America a muscle-bound man's appearance silently declares "No! Not me! I do not have AIDS." Often times true, sometimes false. And sometimes the real statement is simply "Pick me, because I'm the most attractively packaged."

These free association ideas were intended to encourage you to think outside the box.

We know that if you are overweight your chances of being chased after at a party or when you are out, are not as great as if you can "work" a crowd in a white tee, and a pair of tight fitting jeans. How many of us have been mesmerized upon seeing a brother built like a brick house? No matter what he puts on, or doesn't, this brother will have it going on. Duane and I scanned through hundreds of personal ads on the Internet. Reading personal ads of the brothers who had placed an ad looking for "love" or "sex", we found 95% only wanted "a Black God": someone with the looks and the body that is perfect. Here is an example of the typical ad:

"Sup peeps. This is a shout out to all my tight ass niggas. This here is a tight ass, 24-year-old sexy ass bro. I'm 6', 190 well toned body, bow legged, workout 5 days a week. I have a 9' dick and know how to use it, if needed. Don't hit me back unless you have a current pic. I'm looking for a nigga that is fine as I am, on the DL, masculine and. NO FEMS, NO FAT BOYS, or ugly ass niggas wanted. Only fine ass bro's need to apply.

158

If he and the Internet were around in 1950 he may have asked only for Negro gentlemen able to pass the old brown paper bag test. Will less rude, more courteous public discourse appear by 2050?

"I love to see big brothers out at the clubs or pride events. They are no longer staying in the background. Chubby fellas are stepping up and saying look at me. I'm big and I'm beautiful. Fuck you gym rats if you don't like it," says Duane. Those brothers no longer feel that they are not worthy of love. There are men out there who can appreciate a brother for more than the outside packaging. Beauty comes and beauty goes.

That said, Dr. Terry Mason, Chief Urologist at Chicago's Mercy Hospital and spokesman for the National Cancer Institute's "Eat 5 to 9 A Day" health program is concerned with the alarming rise in cancer among African-American men. The National Cancer Institute cites these facts:

1. Black men are about one and one-half times more likely to die prematurely from cancer than Caucasian men.

2. An estimated one-third of all deaths from cancer are related to dietary risk factors. A diet that is low in saturated fats, and contains 5 to 9 servings of fruits and vegetables each day, plays a key role in maintaining good health.

3. Heart disease is the leading cause of death in the USA.

4. Overweight and obesity are the second leading causes of preventable death in the USA.

5. Black men between the ages of 35 and 44 have over twice the rate of death from heart disease than Caucasian men.

6. Left untreated, hypertension (high blood pressure) can damage kidneys and lead to stroke, heart attack and heart failure.

7. Blacks have the highest rate of hypertension in the world, affecting more than one out of every three.

8. The frequency of diabetic eye disease is 40% to 50% higher in Blacks compared with Caucasians in the USA.

9. Approximately 90% to 95% of Blacks with diabetes have "type 2 diabetes" a type that usually develops in

adults and is treatable with the 5 to 9 diet, exercise and annual check-ups with your MD.

10. Being overweight increases the risk for heart disease, stroke, diabetes, and some cancers.

The National Cancer Institute recommends eating 5 to 9 servings of fruits and vegetables every day to reduce the risk for cancer, heart disease, hypertension, diabetes and other diseases, and to maintain good health. Data shows that Black men, ages 35 to 50 on average eat only 3.5 servings of fruits and vegetables a day: less than half of the 9 servings recommended for men. According to the most recent estimates, Blacks eat fewer servings of fruits and vegetables than any other racial or ethnic group.

Come on Brothers! Now that we know better, we can do better than that. We have the power to choose tangerines, grapes and pears over candy bars. We can choose to snack on a banana, a box of raisins, or cashews instead of a bag of chips. Have yogurt or strawberries or cantaloupe for breakfast instead of a doughnut. Drink orange juice instead of soda pop. Learn to appreciate and enjoy the taste of coffee or tea with one teaspoon or less of sugar.

Instead of just chicken and rice, or just beef and potatoes, be sure to add on some good ole' collard greens, corn on the cob, okra, peas, green beans, or other nutritious green and yellow vegetables, or a fresh salad with every dinner. An apple a day keeps the doctor away! When the munchies come on strong, pig out on popcorn, celery sticks, or carrot stalks. A great way to exercise is to walk. 2000 steps every day is ideal. That's about eight city blocks. Do ten pushups a day, every day for a week. The next week do 15 pushups a day, the third week do 20 pushups a day. Continue this pattern, and before you know it you will be up to 50 or 75 a day. Do this gradual increase with other exercises also.

Same gender loving men always have known that to keep man to man sex hot, hot, hot; eat fish, as well as scrambled eggs, oysters, vitamins with a zinc supplement; and drink lots of cranberry juice. There are standard health warnings we would be remiss not to reprint. Do not drink and drive under the influence of alcohol and/or any recreational or prescription drug. At your future parties keep tabs on who will be the designated drivers. Take the car key from a friend you know is too drunk to drive: then call a taxi cab, or make sure they have fare to get on the bus or subway. Wear safety belts each and every time you drive, even for short distances. Insist that all passengers in the car buckle up, with children in the back seat. Cigarette smoking causes cancer. At $4 a pack, smoking one pack a day burns up $1460 a year. Stop smoking today and you get health benefits within one hour: lower blood pressure and better circulation. Your partner gets to breathe air free of second-hand smoke, a carcinogen. The money you save could buy a new compact car every 10 years. Choose to give your health staying power. Eat 5 to 9 servings of vegetables and fruits a day and choose to give your health staying power!

Chapter 14

WHEN YOUR MAN IS LOCKED UP
"WAITING ON LOVE"

Hope is the pillar of the word.

~*Kanuri proverb*

Joe Little is in love with a brother he met on a popular web site. Although he's only talked face-to-face with him twice in the last five years, Joe swears this dude is the one for him. Joe lives more than 350 miles from the prison where his lover is incarcerated. At first, Joe was only interested in having a pen pal because of all the hell he'd been through in past relationships. However, over the years their relationship has become more serious. According to Joe, Jamal gives him the kind of attention, support, and encouragement he needs just from a phone call. Through countless collect telephone calls, letters and cards Jamal has really taken control of Joe's mind and emotions. Both men enjoy their passionate phone sex, and at times, Jamal gets a little jealous when Joe is not home to answer his collect call. Joe frequently sends money orders, care packages and any other requested items to Jamal. Joe says his friends constantly tell him he's wasting his time and money. They tell him that he's too young, at 32 years old, to wait on a man who may or may not get paroled in 10 years when Jamal's first hearing with the parole board is set. Joe says that it is his business, and friends shouldn't worry or lose sleep over his romantic choices.

Joe Little is not the only one stuck on "thug love": choosing to date a man in jail or in prison. Loving inmates can be very risky. Most will have many "lovers" strung out across the country. They get money orders and care packages from each of them. Joe thinks he is Jamal's only lover. James knows several ex-offenders who told him that they had a form letter that they used for all of the lonely gay men they contacted. The inmates promised love and dick when they were released, and played these trusting men like a piano. The same letter with the same hard core thug sex fantasies went out to many men, all feeling hopeful for a future with this playa. At least the phone sex, and sex fantasies in letters were 100% safe sex, in terms of STD transmission.

Keep in mind, these men have nothing but time on their hands. Most have mastered how to use people to get what they want out of them. James says, "It amazes me how brothers who are recently released from the criminal 'just-us' system, will use another man for sex for pay, all while trying to keep his family together." There are hundreds of halfway houses in the United States that are full of eligible, good-looking brothers. Most will be released one day. Nationwide about 2,300 inmates got out each weekday in 2003. Most upon release will not have jobs, or even a place to stay after they do their time. They will be looking for someone to take care of them. Don't you become one of those individuals who will end up bitter and hurt because you let your guards down, and become locked up in your own cell of love gone badly.

Some thugged-out inmates will do anything they can to get all the cheddar (money) they can get added to their commissary books, or to keep care packages rolling in. If that means telling a lonely brother what he wants to hear, then so be it. Not only do you have to be on emotional alert with these cats, there are some health risks to consider also.

We've all heard horror stories of men getting gang raped while in correctional custody. Almost all prison rapes occur without the use of latex condoms. Many states refuse to give inmates condoms for consensual sex between inmates; falsely reasoning that not distributing condoms discourages men from having sex. So if your inmate lover does get a chance to see the light of day, and gets released from the slammer – asking him to take an HIV/AIDS test would be wise. Actually, you should be doing this with anybody, whether they have been in jail or not.

A large percentage of African-American men in prison are there for possession or sale of drugs. Excessive demands for you to send him money orders is a red flag warning that he is buying drugs in the joint. That in turn may indicate he's affiliated with the gang which controls the prison's drug traffic. Will he deplete your bank account upon his release to enrich his pusher? If he tells you he's a "neutron" that means he is not affiliated with any particular gang. Most states have a department of corrections web site you can visit online. Go there with his inmate identification number, date of birth, and/or first and last name, and you can usually get accurate information. A description of crimes he was convicted of, and the dates of custody, estimated date of release and length of parole are available to the public. With the mittimus number posted, you can visit the office of the state's attorney in the county where the crime was committed. That office has detailed records of the trial. If he told you he's locked up for stealing cars, and court records show he beat an elderly lady with a tire iron, you have knowledge he's a violent liar. That gives you power to choose to terminate the relationship, or not, if you think he is repentant, remorseful and ready to live in peace and harmony.

With more African-American men in prison than in college in the USA it is admirable to try to help brothers readjust into the free world. If you cannot work with ex-offenders in a personal relationship, perhaps consider lobbying Congress to legalize marijuana, to decriminalize drugs, or to promote better, more effective addiction recovery services. On a state level, encourage local legislators to vote for laws to expunge the records of those who have served their time, but have trouble getting jobs because of convictions that happened decades ago. It does seem that in these times the most egregious of institutionalized racism takes the form of the so-called war on drugs. When children are eight years old in big city public schools, society is willing to spend $7000 a year to educate them. But when they become 18, society is willing to spend over $25,000 a year to jail them. The cost of incarcerating two of our teenagers could hire a full time drug addiction specialist or a remedial education teacher to help them. It is as if America hated racial integration so much, it is abusing prisons to keep society as segregated as possible.

Anyway, a word of wisdom when it comes to dating men behind bars: keep both eyes wide open and don't be anybody's fool.

Chapter 15

LOVE CRIMES
"TEN WAYS TO KILL A RELATIONSHIP"

Every man who wishes to master his house must first master his emotions.

~Egyptian proverb

Problems will come and go in all relationships. Many people have this false idea that love means no conflict, no problems, no disagreements. But think about it. If you have minor problems and disagreements with your family and friends – and these people are some of the closest to you – why wouldn't you have a few tiffs with your lover? Face the facts; there will be disagreements and differences of opinion in your relationship. How you choose to deal with these situations will speak to how committed you are to your partner.

If you want to start your relationship on a strong foundation, you have to do more than hope and wish. You have to work hard at it every day. You have to realize it is not just about you, that you now are sharing your life with another person. You have to learn to bend, give in and be open to him. You have to learn to break some bad habits and continue to be on top of what you say and what you do that were said and done differently when you were single and free. The minute we align ourselves with someone else, we have to adjust because it is not all about us anymore.

The Golden Rule is simple: treat other people as you would want to be treated, not to treat others any way you feel like it. There are several things that can put the brakes on your relationship faster than a speeding locomotive. Here we go:

1. OPERATE WITHOUT ANY GROUND RULES.

If you want to go nowhere fast, operate your relationship in the cosmic world of assumptions. This is the place where you are the center of the universe and you make the mistake of thinking he views a relationship the same way you do. How many times have you heard a variation of: I shouldn't have to tell the person I love what to do. If he loved me he'd just do it!

Believe it or not, we have to teach our lover how to treat us, and how to give us the love we desire. We can't just assume our lover knows what's going on in our heart and in our mind. Hell, some of us don't even know what's going on in these intimate places because we've never taken the time to reflect and to contemplate our heart of hearts. We choose instead to

175

go through the motions of life on autopilot. If this is the case for you, you may want to put thoughts of going into a relationship on hold, until you can get your own act together.

Think of ground rules for a relationship like a Fortune 500 company's mission statement. Nothing successful operates without a plan or system in place and your relationship is no different. Will your relationship be open? If so, does "open" mean the same thing to you and your partner? For some, open means the two partners can still date and have sex with other people independent of one another. For others open means the couple will allow other sexual partners to join the couple in a three way, but independent dating with the third person is forbidden. You and your partner should sit down and discuss that concept, before it causes major problems in your relationship. Will you live together or not? How much of your love relationship will be disclosed: to family relatives, friends and co-workers? These are some things that have to be up on the table for clear, open, honest discussion from the start.

2. NEVER TAKE FOR GRANTED THAT YOUR PARTNER KNOWS HOW YOU FEEL ABOUT HIM.

You need to tell him how you feel, and how special he is to you. All the things you told him and shared with him when you were trying to get with him should be on going. Always keep up the chase. The more time you spend with him the more comfortable you feel, as you grow accustomed to his presence in your life. Have the same attitudes and behaviors as when you were first dating him, trying to make a good first impression. It does not help that the stress of everyday life: working our 9 to 5's, paying bills and contributing to community service can, at times, cause us to loose focus. But love needs to be nurtured. Do not try to put on a false front. You should make it a priority to find ways to tell your partner he's loved and appreciated often. If you cannot remember the last time you told your significant other "I love you" or cannot recall the last romantic thing you did for him to put your love into action, you're in trouble and you had better get to work to keep the flames of passion burning.

3. NEVER TAKE A PHONE NUMBER FROM ANOTHER MAN, AND NOT TELL YOUR PARTNER ABOUT IT.

If someone gives you his or her number, even if it is a business connection, you should share that with your partner. It isn't worth keeping a secret. Doing so will create confusion. Keeping your lover abreast of who you communicate with is an honest approach.

4. FAILURE TO BE A MAN OF YOUR WORD: IF YOU SAY YOU ARE GOING TO DO SOMETHING, THEN YOU DO IT!

No one wants a man with a bag of empty promises. Keep your dates and appointments for quality times with your lover. If you cannot, be very sure to communicate this to him well in advance of any cancellation. Just do not show up late and act like nothing is wrong. Plus be honest. Never ever tell your partner you're going one place and you end up someplace else.

5. NEVER GO OFF BY YOURSELF AT A SOCIAL FUNCTION, CLUB, BAR, ETC WITH ANOTHER MAN, TO WHERE YOUR PARTNER CANNOT FIND YOU.

Then when he does find you, he finds you talking to

another brother, someone he does not know. When he approaches you, you start acting nervous and it shows that you were not having a conversation about your favorite CD or the latest movie. When you have a partner, his needs and feelings should rank highest on your list. Likewise he should take your needs into account before those of other people in his life. Never disrespect your partner in public. Use constructive criticism in private.

6. NEVER LET JEALOUSY AND ENVY GET THE BEST OF YOU.

Watching how these emotions play out in SGL relationships could be interesting if it were not so tragic and sad. In the SGL community jealousy and envy sometimes arise from fear of losing our partners to another. Sometimes those emotions stem from low self-esteem or baggage from past relationships that we need to deal with before we can move on with another person. Sometimes we will carry stuff into new relationships that will cause major problems. From being over protective, to being unable to trust anyone, many of us have issues that we have to resolve.

179

7. HAVE NO LIFE OF YOUR OWN.

If you are constantly waiting by the phone for your man to call or for him to swing by to sex you up, then you are cheating yourself out of a full and healthy life. You would be surprised by how much more you have to give to a partner when you have other goals, activities and social networks to occupy your time. If you are not a social butterfly, try reaching out to family and close friends. The bottom line is to maintain a life outside of the relationship.

8. IGNORE WHAT YOU HEAR.

You have to listen to your partner's needs and requests. Failure to pay attention to these things because you are too busy wanting to do things your way will drive your man away.

9. REFUSAL TO RELEASE.

It is important for you and your partner to regularly take inventory of the relationship. Find a time interval that works best for you and him, whether it is every year, six months or some shorter interval. This release time should be done in an environment where egos are put aside, and ears are wide open. It is a time out to listen; to the good, the bad and the ugly that may exist in your relationship. Be careful not to turn it into a complaint session, but a productive conversation where you can discuss feelings, thoughts and ideas.

10. PREVENTING HIM FROM BEING HIMSELF.

No matter how fine you may be or think you are, you can only control what you do. You cannot change another person. So know what you're getting into as quickly as you can. Let him be himself. Life is short and then you die. We only get one life. There are no second chances when it comes to this beautiful gift God has given us. So, live every day as if it is your last, because it could be. At any given time, you can read in the daily newspaper and see how young people are dying of AIDS or dropping dead as the result of other health troubles. Others go to work, only to end up dead because someone chose to "go postal" on the job and they were in the wrong place at the wrong time. Tomorrow is not promised to any of us. Treat people the way you want to be treated. Be honest with yourself, and show some love to everyone on the street. When you have on your fly gear, and know you are looking good it is a good thing to smile and say hello to a brother who may not have arrived and has less than you have.

Some of us can't smile because we are hurting inside. Some of us live a double life that becomes stressful and we take our hurt out on each other. Those closest to us get it the worst when we act out. Your sexuality is only one part of you. Too many of us think we are somehow flawed because of our sexual orientation. We don't realize we have a multi-faceted life. With the embracing of these truths, you can start the process of learning how to uplift your spirit and to be more content with yourself. It is understandable to be mentally stressed. Just don't add to your difficulties by trying to escape them. Do not be the last one to know that addiction has entered your life. We highly recommend Alcoholics Anonymous and/or Narcotics Anonymous. Both groups have helped thousands of people get to the crux of issues that devastate relationships.

Chapter 16

AFTER THE CLUBS, BARS, AND PARTIES

"WHAT ARE YOU GOING TO DO?"

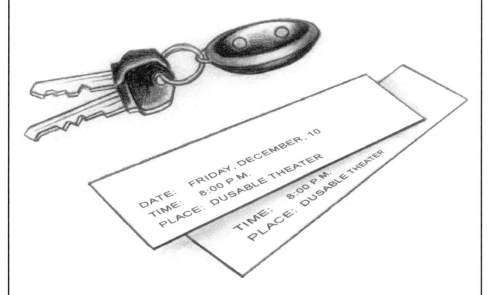

Strategy is better than strength. A good conversation is better than a good bed.

~Hausa proverb

Going to clubs, bars, and other places where men cruise, may put you in an environment that is not good for your relationship. Whether or not this is so depends on how each couple chooses to negotiate club etiquette. While many people may enjoy socializing, dancing and meeting new people – temptation is strong and you have to be honest with yourself. Examine your true motivation for clubbing. Is it to socialize or is it really a meat market for you to shop for your next big, beefy, tasty sexual conquest? If you are naturally sexually aggressive, as most men are, then you are bound to have problems in your relationship. This may be reflected in how you act in the club. Don't get it twisted. You don't have to be on lockdown or stuck up under your partner 24 / 7 / 365. We all need space and time away from our mates. We all want to get out and see if we still have what it takes to turn heads. It makes us feel good to know our game is still on point, especially when over 30 candles are on our birthday cake. For example, some men love to look at and acknowledge a fine hottie when they spot one walking down the street, or rolling into Starbucks to grab a cup of coffee. This is where knowing your mate and having good communication is key. Some couples may choose to work through this issue by honestly communicating with their partner about their roving eyes and what they see.

Now if you or your partner has a problem with the way a stare or glance is exchanged between someone else, that has to be communicated also. Talk about what is creating the displeasure. Is it insecurity? Do you or does your partner view it as a disrespectful form of flirting? It won't pay to assume that everyone thinks about these things in the same way that you think about them. So you can't be afraid to talk it through. Severe jealousy will kill a relationship in the same time Raid kills a roach: quick, fast, and in a hurry. But you cannot cure what is concealed. The situation must be addressed in order for the relationship to work. You and your partner must tackle the underlying issue and come to a solution that will benefit your union. A house divided cannot stand.

Our Puritanical monogamous culture values and validates the one man for one woman until death do you part ideal. Never mind that many heterosexual couples don't think this model works for them. Divorce ends many marriages.

The days of Ozzie and Harriett are long gone. Many same gender loving couples who have been together for any significant time reveal that communicating fantasies and desires about other men outside of the relationship adds a bit of spice and variety to the relationship.

There are several things that Duane and I like to do as a couple. I love to take him out on a date. We like going to a predominately heterosexual club instead of gay clubs. We have more fun and we love dancing with women. At heterosexual clubs or alternative clubs you don't find the attitudes, and the feeling of being in a meat market. At many gay clubs everyone is styling and profiling. No one is talking or trying to meet and greet. There have been only a few Black gay clubs that we have patronized and we left feeling good. One is a popular club we visited in Atlanta while in the Peach State on business. When we got there we were greeted in a warm friendly way. Two really nice brothers at the door didn't present the image of a bouncer. The bartenders were all cool. The brothers in the place, on the patio, and just standing around spoke and offered conversation. When we can find an establishment that makes us feel good about being out, and spending our money, then we will continue to go to that place and support that establishment.

It would be great if someone would open a SGL friendly place where we could go right after work. I hate going out at 1 or 2 in the morning. I guess I'm getting to the point in my life where I would rather be in bed with my dude, than go out to a club after midnight. It would be nice to go to an upscale bar right after work, have some drinks, socialize, network, listen to some nice music, and then go home. Some couples are not big on going to clubs, bars, sex parties, and other gathering spots that men use to meet other men. Instead some opt to spend their time doing other things such as traveling, entertaining friends and family at home, spending quality time with each other or pursuing individual interests such as volunteer activities and other civic and community service-related projects. "We both have attended a few sex parties, bathhouses, and were the last ones to leave," says Duane. "We both knew coming to the table we weren't virgins, we had a history, and we were experienced. But we both knew we were tired of all that, and wanted someone to come home to and to spend long meaningful nights with." What we discovered was a big world out there, which offered more than a life of weekend parties and bar hopping. We turned our attention to us, and we love being together," Duane said as James nodded in agreement. "To see us you would think we had just met. We can be in a crowded room full of people, and we will have a deep conversation, as if we are the only people in the room. And this is after being together over eight years."

Once you find that special person, you know you want to put your all into making it work. It is important for you to learn how to do things together as a couple. But also trust that when you are separated your partner will give you the utmost respect.

Chapter 17

TRADE
"DEALING WITH TEMPORARY FIXES TO BEING ALONE?"

He may say he loves you, wait and see what he does for you.

~Senegalese proverb

What would we do without trade? Trade is a man who will accept cash, a place to live, a ride into town or a half-smoked joint in exchange for sex. How else could we get through those long spells of not having sex? There were days when we jacked off watching erotic videos, porno magazines, or were online with our web camera at home. Sultry hot August nights of cruising the parks and adult bookstores were the times many of us felt like we needed trade. On the surface, these dudes are pretty low maintenance and brutally honest about what their demands are. They are only interested in what you can do for them materially and monetarily.

These men refuse to have any emotional connection with you, even though in the back of your mind you may have a hidden wish for them to love you, (or at least allow you 24-hour access to the zipper on his pants). What trade loves is that your money will buy: cigarettes, 40 ounces of malt liquor, crack, cocaine or heroin. A man in this group does not really care about you. A man in this group does not have a desire to get to know you, unless he's going to get something out of interacting with you. He simply views you as a business transaction. You come to him to be serviced and he is willing to do just that, but it is going to cost you!

It's a fact that the SGL life can, at times, be lonely and isolating. Unlike our heterosexual counterparts, we have fewer outlets to socialize as we network with other men. We can clearly relate to the late Phyllis Hyman when the sultry R&B legend declared, "I can't stand this living all alone." The temptation to get caught up in trade is great because paying for affection; even when we know it is feeding addiction, and it is too superficial and temporary to be satisfying, is for some a lot better than not having any affection at all. We see this play out with some of our friends. Doesn't this scenario sound familiar?

A friend of yours meets a new piece (a.k.a. trade) he's cruised in the park or picked up off the streets. He takes him home, cleans him up, and then introduces him to you as his new man. Where did this brother come from? Did he just arrive from the planet Mars as a perfect lover?

Trouble in paradise is soon on the horizon when the drama starts. This is when "Mr. Perfect" beats down your friend or steals his car, cash and credit cards while he's at work. You hear about it over the phone, as your friend is distraught and upset. When you ask him how did this happen? Your boy responds with that played-out quote, "I just tried to help a brother out." Yeah, right! Why doesn't he just tell the truth? He is too proud to say that the fire of lust in his heart put smoke in his eyes and he was blinded: by horniness or loneliness, or perhaps a combination of both, and he just got caught up. Making your move too soon, with limited information about trade, can be emotionally and physically dangerous. We've visited too many friends in the hospital who were almost killed because they allowed trade to enter their life. For just one night of hot steamy sweaty passion, the brothers get stabbed. Trade is filled with deeply internalized self-hatred that is often acted-out violently, with little warning when trade is drunk or high. The lesson here is very clear. Do not let your little head make your love life decisions. As for dealing with loneliness, here are a few tips: You have got to stop beating yourself up about being single! Snap out of it! It does not help the psyche to constantly dwell on what you don't have. The more you concentrate on the absence of a partner, the more negative your thinking becomes as self-doubt creeps into your life. Your well developed dating standards fly out the window as you begin to settle and compromise for less than what you know you deserve just so you can say you have a man. Being lonely and horny, you give up on the long-term prospect for Mr. Right, and develop unrealistic hopes for Mr. Right-Now.

Take a look at the man in the mirror. Self-reflection on all the blessings in your life is a positive way to evaluate what's going on inside of you. At some point you have to address why loneliness is getting the best of you and causing you to make unwise decisions. These foolish decisions may include: your choice to constantly be taken advantage of, your refusal to have adequate boundaries and limits when it comes to how others treat or mistreat you, or your apparent willingness to take risky life-threatening dare-devil chances. You may find it valuable to talk with a therapist or psychologist who specializes in sexual orientation issues. (Before you say it, NO – seeing a therapist or psychologist is not just for the insane). There are a number of self-help books that can help you.

Pursue hobbies, take self-improvement classes, learn a foreign language; read a newspaper every day, read a magazine every week, and read a good book every month. There is some truth to the adage that idle time is the devil's workshop. Too much time spent being unproductive can bring out the worst in many of us. Love, affection, adoration and companionship can come from plenty sources other than a $20 hustler in your bed. We know you may be saying to yourself, there is nothing like love shared by two men. But there are other ways to feel special. You will be surprised how much better you can feel about yourself when you start sharing your time, talent and resources with other people who really need a helping hand in life. Volunteering for civic service is one way to get the lonely monkey off your back. Thousands of young African-American men out there need a tutor or mentor. If kids and teenagers are not your most favorite people in the world, many senior citizens could benefit from your help. If there is a social cause, political campaign or community service group that speaks to your heart, you could try to devote your spare time each week or month to it.

194

Maybe you'd feel more comfortable helping other people, after you have helped yourself. In that case, try going back to school to get that degree which could lead to a better paying job. Take up that art class or fitness program you've been putting off. A temporary fix to a major problem is like putting a bandage on a broken arm. Using trade to get over an emotional hump may not help in the long run if you really truly want sincere male intimacy.

Chapter 18

LONG DISTANCE RELATIONSHIPS

"THEY CAN WORK, IF..."

Absence makes the heart forget.

~Kenyan proverb

Did you ever hear how one of your friends or associates met a fly guy during the Washington, D. C. Memorial Day Weekend Black Pride event and love at first sight developed?

Your friend may have been ready to pack all his worldly possessions and move to Huntsville, Alabama or some place 500 miles away from where he lives.

You cannot believe he's seriously contemplating how he will: quit his job, break his lease, (or move out of his mama's house) and set up shop with this newfound love---all because of a one night of hard core frottage sex (see chapter 20) and some good conversation. PLEASE!!!!

This happens to many SGL men who enter into a cycle of a high speed, crash and burn styles of relationship building.

Soon the desire to explore a long distance relationship is created during a holiday's travel, professional conference or out of quick one weekend get-a-ways from your hometown.

There is no thought about phone bills until the first one comes in at $413 and is 15 pages thick. Or there may come a day when the money may get funny and there's no money around to buy round trip tickets to visit your distant lover for those sexy weekend trysts.

After a few weeks of giving it a try: the phone calls stop coming in everyday. E-mail messages that were once sent daily now cease and you are getting calls from friends urging you to go out and revisit the local sights and pleasures of men in your own backyard.

Soon what was once a perfect brotha, whom you had to be with for life, is a wet dream memory until the next Pride event in Los Angeles, Atlanta or Chicago. If you really want to stay in touch, a practical thing is to write letters. The post office sends them anywhere in the country for just 37 cents. Handwritten letters these days are rare enough to be very unique and special to someone who gets them from you. It could have been beautiful. It could have been a love for life had the distance not been so great.

On the other hand, there are some brothers who meet that special person and the rigors of distance are not too overwhelming to keep them apart. Through sacrifice, they vow to be together.

No matter what is going on in their individual lives, the two men ultimately take the plunge and decide they will be together in one city under one roof—A move Duane and I opted to pursue.

JAMES AND DUANE DECIDE TO LIVE AS ONE AS TOLD BY JAMES

We did it. I was living in the south; my partner was in NYC. I was comfortable and happy with my life in Atlanta. When I met him, I was not planning to move. But, when the love bug bit me, all I wanted to do was to be with him. (And he felt that same way.) We started talking about it. We weighed all of our options; we looked at several cities that would work for both of us. We made a plan, set some realistic goals and set dates to make the move happen. One good thing that worked in our favor was since I was self employed; I could live anywhere in the country. As long as I could get to an airport, it was all good. We agreed on Chicago. It was the perfect city for both of our needs, both personally and professionally.

We decided on a city, then we started making our goal a reality. I was on a month- to- month lease; he was at the end of his yearly lease. His place was too small for both of us, so we started looking at a new place that would be our place. But, we also wanted a trail period to see if we could live together. So for three months we lived in loft together and maintained his apartment. This gave us a way out. If it didn't work, at least he still had his place to keep, and I could move on. We decided to share the expenses on both places, and make a go of it.

After 3 months, there was no doubt that we could live together, and started our search for a permanent place.

So my advice to you is if you both put equal amounts of time into making a long distance relationship work, it will.

Chapter 19

To Each His Own

"Love in black and white, take the chip off your shoulder"

If the heart is sad, tears will flow.

~African proverb

This is a subject that some brothas fight with internally. They ask; *Should I cross the street and get a man of another color such as a Jewish, Australian, Russian or Korean lover?*

The motivation behind this thought-process is usually an attitude that there are not enough suitable African-American men available. (Sounds like African-American woman's dilemma, doesn't it?)

Being with a man of your own race is challenging and an interracial romance may add another layer to an already complex lifestyle—yet it can work, again, if the two men involved have a strong passion and desire to make it work.

Some of us don't see color, we just see the character of the person's heart.

Some brothas go for the money. For example, some brothas will date old, wrinkled white men so they can be taken care of.

How many times have you been out at a nice restaurant

and seen a fine brother in tailored clothes with a sad looking white man. The white man is; either old as the hills, out of shape or just a real life troll. You say to yourself, "he's gotta call a trailer park home." And you ask yourself.... WHY?

The fine brother won't even look at you. Don't try to speak to him: you may get the look that says, "I am a colored boy today, a living breathing Oreo." You may get the look that says "I'm with my man from Tashkent, Uzbekistan, and you wouldn't understand."

It is a mystery to me why some African-American men who date white men won't give another brotha the time of day if he is not fine, well paid, and have other qualities that he will not demand from his white interests. These double standards don't make any sense. Perhaps it's the acting out of self-hatred, internalized racism.

"I personally dated, no let me keep it real, was fucking a white boy when I was in college," says James. "The sex was off da' chain, and the white boy could suck a dick. Plus, he didn't care about anything but getting penetrated every chance he got."

205

"At his parents house, while they were sleep, in his mom's flower garden, or at work. (FYI: We worked together at this grocery store, and he would want me to sex him up after the store closed.) We would screw in the meat freezer, or on top of the wholesale buyer's desk. Yea, dude was a freak like that. But, it was strictly sex."

If you feel that you are going to have to get you a white dude in order to find true love, then please make sure that you don't loose who you are and where you come from. Don't look down on your friends and other brothers when you are out with your white trade, because a lot of brothers are not feeling you, because you can do better, than to be a Tom with a white boy. Also, please don't let your white boy disrespect your people.

Sometimes white boys will tell you that "your people," need this and that, and "your people" would be better off if they were to do this and did that.

You don't have to sell out to keep him happy and interested in you. Just keep it real.

Noted national author and LGBT Community activist

Keith Boykin writes on his web site (www.keithboykin.com). A friend, a successful Black gay professional, often complained to me that he could not find Black men of his "caliber". "Black gay men", he said, were often uneducated and not as successful as he. After searching for a year or two, he settled down in a relationship with a white man with a blue- collar job. It seems my friend was actually less interested in his partner's caliber than in his race. Why couldn't he just tell the truth? He did not want to date a Black man. He wanted a white man instead. To catch his eye, a Black man would have to be twice as gorgeous and twice as successful as an average white man. Keith wraps up his story by saying, "What concerns me is when Black gay men consciously choose not to date other Black men. I can understand when a Black man dates outside of his race. I cannot understand when a Black man refuses to date within his race. Such exclusion, it seems to me, is rooted in a deep self hatred".

It is a mystery to me why some Black men who date white men won't give another brother the time of day if he is not fine, well paid and in possession of other qualities that he will not demand from his white interests. These double standards don't make any sense says Duane.

A STORY FROM A WHITE MAN'S PERSPECTIVE ON INTERRACIAL DATING:

I feel that when Black men see me with my Black lover they get upset because I have someone that they want. I am giving my Black lover the respect and love that he could not find from another Black man. I did not chase him or do anything to get him to fall in love with me. I did what I would do with any potential mate of any racial or ethnic group.

My lover told me that he was tired of all the games and issues Black men bring into relationships. He said that Black men he met are confused about their sexual orientation. Many only want sex: no commitment, just sex. My lover was tired of the bull. He wanted a good life, a nice home and a partner who listens to him. He has felt the stares and has heard the talk from his friends about us. He knows he can't be with me without the negative talk from his family. He dares not invite me to church. When I take him around my family and friends, they love him and accept us as a couple. He is accepted as a professional man with good manners who is treating me like I should be treated. I think that the Black community needs to be less hostile about interracial dating, because we are not hurting anyone by being in love with each other. Your men are crossing over without being lured by money, status or all the other things that a lot of Black men think is the reason why they are with us, and not with them.

Robert G.   Boston, Massachusetts

Chapter 20

FROTTAGE

"KEEP STD OUT OF YOUR RELATIONSHIP"

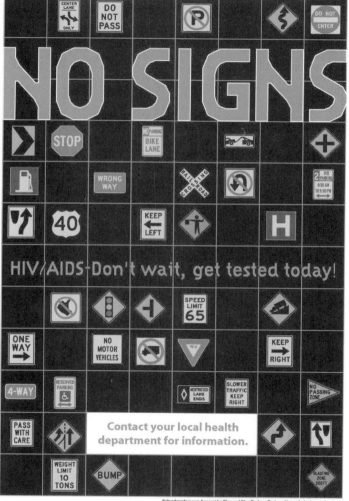

*One lie ruins a thousand truths, however
in every false step there is something good.*
~Ghanaian and Moroccan proverb

Frottage is the rubbing of your penis against your partner's penis, leg, belly, arm, foot or anywhere until you achieve ejaculation. Frottage also is called body grinding, humping, slick-legging, and friction. Face to face, phallus to phallus try it well oiled, lying down, and it will prove to be intensely pleasurable. Standing up in the shower, both of you covered with thick soapy lather, getting your freak on with frot is hot, hot, hot. Try it with lube, between your partner's legs, under his scrotum, while deep soul kissing. Frottage is not just foreplay. Same gender lovemaking with the practice of frottage is going safely all the way.

The decision never to have anal sex in any position, with no exceptions.

The decision never to have anal sex in any position, with no exceptions, has given many brothers the ability to stay both sexually active and free of HIV well into middle age and beyond. It is a clear and non-negotiable boundary. Usually much creative thinking for alternative sexual expressions results from making this choice. Why would or why should this choice never to have anal sex be made?

Condoms are about 97% effective. That sounds pretty good for safer sex. But would you drive down the interstate highway knowing that your car's brakes are going to fail 3% of the time? No! You would put that car in the shop right away if its brakes weren't 100% reliable. When dealing with a virus that can cause life-threatening diseases, and you know that once you get HIV you have it for life: many people find a 3% condom failure risk unacceptable.

Your skin is waterproof. If you do not know whether your partner is HIV positive or not, you can enjoy a frottage session with him, with or without wearing a condom. When he ejaculates onto your skin, unless you have an open wound at the exact spot where his semen lands, you cannot get the virus. You have poured many kinds of liquids onto your skin over the course of your life; dish-washing detergent, window cleaner with ammonia, and all kinds of wet surfaces when walking on bare feet. You have touched with the skin of your hands all kinds of wet surfaces while not wearing gloves. With soap and water it all washed off, and you suffered no ill effects.

213

By contrast, the inner lining of the rectum absorbs liquid. With anal intercourse, hundreds of blood capillaries, too small to see without a microscope, are ruptured. The damage from that abrasion gives the HIV virus direct access to your bloodstream. Many men get drunk or high before having sex, and may therefore neglect to put on a condom. In some instances the rubber can fall off if the inserting partner goes soft soon after climax. And in instances when an oil-based lubricant like Vaseline or hair grease is used for screwing, the rubber can break. These troubles are minimized in a relationship in which your partner cares about whether you become infected. Often in real life, many men screw and get screwed with partners that they do not know, or who does not care. Choosing never to accept the 3% chance may be the most important decision of your life, or your premature death. In a LGBT community that claims to honor diversity, there is some resistance you may encounter to being a "frot buddy" instead of being a "fuck buddy". SGL men into anal penetrating sex sometimes will pressure men into frot by saying, "you don't really love me if you won't let me fuck you." Sometimes an anal receptive will attempt to pressure men into frot by saying, "if you really love me, you would fuck me." Perhaps the best bet in these situations is to compromise and use a finger, dildo or vibrator. This is certainly a conversation to have with your partner long before the sexual action gets hot and heavy. Use a condom on a dildo, and then discard the condom and use another condom before the dildo is used on another person.

Meanwhile some men into frot are clear, strong and unequivocal in their opposition to any anal sex at all, even with dildos or gloved fingers. That most strident position alarms SGL men who have enjoyed anal sex, with condoms, for years. They say advocates of frottage, who also are against anal sex, are the radical gay Taliban sex police, oppressive to men who love anal sex in every position.

The American Journal of Health Behavior reported on a study of 224 males seeking treatment at a Birmingham, AL STD clinic for low-income patients. Despite knowing or suspecting they had a disease and understanding that not using condoms increased their likelihood of contracting another one, 66% of the men with a primary partner said they did not plan future condom use. 33% of the men without a primary partner said they would not use condoms. These men mainly said they did not like condoms because they did not want to have to rely on a partner's cooperation, and that condoms made sex feel unnatural. According to Univ. of AL professor Diane Grimley, the study's lead author, men in more intimate relationships were the least likely to use condoms, wanting their partners to feel they were committed to the relationship. Rather than use condoms, many men preferred to take their chances and seek treatment if they became infected. In Alabama, Blacks made up roughly 60% of AIDS patients since 1984, but only 25% of the AL population.

Back in the day, when you would buy a mattress, it would come with a tag on it saying, "DO NOT REMOVE UNDER PENALTY OF LAW". When I was 13 years old I felt a guilty pleasure in ripping that tag off my mattress after midnight late one night. I covered up that crime with a fitted sheet. Until just now, nobody has ever known. And so it is with whether you do or don't do whatever sexual activity you desire. (See chapter 3 on Free Will). When you are with a consenting adult in private, mostly it just ain't nobody's business if you do.

Over the entire course of human history, humans have evolved and adapted. Saliva in the mouth has always been the body's first line of defense against germs that would enter the mouth. Saliva is underrated as a front line of defense in the battle against HIV. Also underrated and underreported in HIV prevention messages is the power of the light bulbs. Fellatio clearly permits the catcher to observe and to examine the pitcher's bat and balls. Common sense says partners in any romantic rendezvous should care about each other's health and well-being. With the light on in your bedroom, or when you shower with your partner before sex, what you see is what you get. If either partner sees an unexplained sore or rash in the genital area both are obligated by love. The pitcher needs to decline to have sex until completely cured. The catcher has the right to refuse sex until any sore or abrasion or rash is completely cured. Doing it in the dark is a perfect way to find your lips on herpes sores you would have seen if you had left the light on.

217

Anyone with even half a brain knows that there is more than an apples and oranges difference between a mouth and a butt. For example, butts don't have teeth. Even if someone tried to be a medical miracle by growing teeth in their butt, you would never know. This is because the butt is a place where the sun won't shine. You cannot see and observe cuts, abrasions, herpes sores etc. up in there, up in there, even with your bedroom lamp on. The lone fact that you cannot see obvious signs of infection by non HIV STD (like herpes and syphilis) makes leaving the lights on the better choice.

When you are the oral sex catcher, never brush your teeth just before having sex, toothbrush bristles can cause temporary abrasions along the gums. Wait a couple hours after brushing before having oral sex. Eat creamy peanut butter sandwiches for safer sex? Yes. Just as putty seals leaks in concrete, you can let the food putty that stays between teeth after you eat bread provide a back up to your natural saliva defense against germs. In a healthy man, ejaculated semen is sterile with salt water, trace amounts of protein and more vitamin C per unit volume than orange juice: in essence its harmless. The logical catcher in an oral sex relationship would pick an HIV negative partner. Each partner ought to honestly disclose his HIV status to his partner. The pitcher in an oral sex relationship can also say "open wide, deep throat" and take a look see at what he is getting into. Before the onset of the worldwide AIDS pandemic, the lives of SGL people seemed so carefree. There was no discussion of risky sexual behavior. Before we had heard of HIV, the last thing on anybody's mind was wearing condoms.

These days and times, because anal penetration without a condom is the sexual act most likely to transmit HIV, frottage is recommended for sex without a condom. Some men do not like the feeling of a condom, while others neglect to wear one for various reasons.

Lovemaking is a beautiful thing, that's even better when you have all your health and strength. Why chance it? Yes, condoms do reduce risk of HIV transmission, and do help you avoid other sexually transmitted diseases. Perhaps the sensible pre-requisite for anal sex is that you are into a long-term monogamous relationship and you know you know your partner's HIV status, and he knows yours.

JL King, national HIV prevention activist and author states that many people do not know their HIV status. Many people have never been tested, and many do not want to know their HIV status. King states that many brothers get into sexual relationships with other men, without ever asking that important question, "Do you know your HIV status?". They assume that the person is not HIV positive and go into a sexual relationship without using protection. King says that he knows many brothers who have never been tested, and they are having unprotected sex with a lot of people. He said that one of his friends told him he will never wear a condom; "don't like the feeling of them". Another friend told me the other day, that he knows he is HIV positive, and he tells his sexual partners that he is positive; and they still want to have "raw" sex with him (RAW means the same as "bareback", sex without use of a condom). He said he has anally penetrated heterosexual men, married to women and many single SGL men without a condom and he achieved orgasm in them, and they did not care, "To me this is crazy, but it is reality," King says. God forbid you get a STD because your partner went out and picked up a little bug that can be cured with a shot or a pill. But lets pray that you never get HIV because your partner puts your life and his life at risk.

If this does happen and you find out that he is HIV positive, then you have a big problem on your hands. First, you will go through some mixed feelings. You will be angry because the man you gave your body to now has hurt you. Then you will be mad because the love you have for him will not just disappear. You may want to hurt him, or worse, but you still love him.

What you need to do now is go to see your doctor and get the medical help you need to live as long as you can. You also need to talk to your partner and find out how he got infected. Once you have decided what you want to do next with your life, always remember it is all about you. That you will live, and you will take this lesson as not a time to beat yourself up, but to protect yourself from any more hurt and harm.

TEST YOUR KNOWLEDGE ABOUT HIV/AIDS

1. AIDS stands for:

    A. Acquired infectious death syndrome.

    B. Acquired immune deficiency syndrome.

    C. Acquired invasive diagnosis of the immune system.

2. The world's earliest known case of HIV was found in:

    A. 1959

    B. 1964

    C. 1979

3. How is HIV transmitted?

_____

_____

_____

4. How soon after possible exposure do I wait to get an HIV test?

    A. Three days

    B. Three months

    C. One year

5. How long does it take for HIV to cause AIDS?

    A. Three months

    B. 13 months

    C. Varies from person to person

6. It is (true / false) that only bottoms can contract HIV. For information on HIV and AIDS call the CDC National AIDS Hotline at 1- 800 – 342 – 2437 or 1- 800 – 243 – 7889 (TTY)

ANSWERS TO THE HIV / AIDS QUIZ

1. AIDS stands for B. Acquired immune deficiency syndrome An HIV-infected person receives a diagnosis of AIDS only after developing one of the Center's for Disease Control's defined AIDS indicator illnesses. An HIV-positive person who has not had any serious illness also can receive an AIDS diagnosis on the basis of certain blood tests (CD4+ counts)

2. The world's earliest known case of HIV was found in A. 1959 The earliest known case of HIV was from a blood sample collected in 1959 from a man in Kinshasa, Democratic Republic of Congo. (How he became infected is not known.) Genetic analysis of this blood sample suggests that HIV-1 may have stemmed from a single virus in the late 1940's or early 1950's. We do know that the virus has existed in the USA since at least the mid to late 1970's. From 1979 to 1981 rare

223

types of pneumonia, cancer and other illnesses were being reported by doctors in San Francisco and New York: among a number of gay male patients. These were conditions not usually found in people with healthy immune systems.

3. HIV is transmitted by: The exchange of bodily fluids; blood, semen, vaginal fluid and mammary gland milk, from an infected person, by sharing needles and/or syringes (primarily for drug injection) with someone who is infected. Less commonly (and now very rarely in countries where blood is screened for HIV antibodies), through transfusions of infected blood or blood clotting factors. Babies born to HIV-infected women may become infected before or during birth, or through breast-feeding after birth. Some people fear that HIV might be transmitted in other ways (such as through air, water, or insects). No scientific evidence to support any of these fears has been found. Patterns of HIV cases would be much different if the fears were valid.

4. If you think you've been exposed to HIV, you should get tested about three months from the day you think

you were exposed. The tests commonly used to detect HIV infection actually look for antibodies produced by your body to fight HIV. Most people will develop detectable antibodies within 3 months after infection, the average being 25 days. In rare cases it can take up to 6 months.

5. How long does it take for HIV to cause AIDS? If you answered both B and C you are correct. Since 1992, scientists have estimated that about half the people with HIV develop AIDS within 10 years after becoming infected. This time varies greatly from person to person and can depend on many factors, including the person's prior health status and their health-related behaviors. Today there are medical treatments that can slow down the rate at which HIV weakens the immune system. There are other treatments that can prevent or cure some of the illnesses associated with AIDS. The treatments do not cure AIDS itself. As with other diseases, early detection offers more options for treatment and preventative health care.

6. It is false to assume only bottoms can contract HIV. *Please note: the CDC provides all the facts in the quiz.

The authors cannot stress enough the importance of getting tested. If you test negative, praise God and change the way you have been rolling if you know it has been high-risk sex. If you test HIV positive, get the right medical attention as soon as possible. Then live a long and productive life. Testing positive does not mean the end of your life, but the beginning of a new you.

Chapter 21

DOMESTIC VIOLENCE
"BUT I LOVE HIM TOO MUCH TO LEAVE HIM"

Do not be so much in love that you can't tell when rain comes.

~Kenyan proverb

The time to recognize that things are not working out in your relationship is sooner rather than later. Often a good way to know what a person will do in the future is to look at what they have done repeatedly in the past. Unresolved power and control issues between men can lead to domestic violence. If you saw your parents fight often, and got used to fighting, you may think that's the way love is. Abuse may even stop short of violence and involve coercion, threats, intimidation, or the taking away of your hopes and dreams.

Pay attention to how you really feel, and respond to your first mind when red flags appear. *These are patterns of behavior of abusers:*

1. Threatening physical harm.

2. Depriving you of sleep, food, money, or medical assistance.

3. Hair pulling, biting, pushing, punching, kicking.

4. Isolating you from your family and friends.

5. Intimidation with a weapon.

6. Forcing you to have sex against your will.

7. Threatening to tell your sexual orientation or HIV status to those who would abuse that information.

8. Calling you names that disrespect, in private and in public.

9. Minimizing, denying, or blaming you for the abuse they are doing to you.

10. Being dishonest.

These are patterns of behavior of a person being abused:

1. Blaming yourself for loss of control, extortion of your money, or deprivation of sleep, food or medical care.

2. Denial that you are intimidated, fearful or helpless

3. Minimizing or making excuses for violent acts against you.

4. Feeling you have no one to talk to.

5. Afraid to leave someone who mistreats you.

6. Allowing your property to be damaged or taken.

7. Allowing your pets to be hurt or killed.

8. Thinking the abuser is not responsible for his actions because he is under the influence of alcohol and / or narcotics.

9. Thinking you did something to provoke the violence and you are getting what you deserve.

10. Thinking GLBT domestic violence is part of consensual bondage / discipline or sadist / masochist relationships (which are highly structured, and contain strict preset boundaries).

Know that abusers sense who can be controlled, who is insecure, and who has a heart so on fire they cannot see the red flags through the smoke. Avoid going from one bad relationship to another by first realizing that you must first have a good relationship with yourself. Know that getting involved in a relationship with another person may be delayed until a non-abusive person enters your life.

Even so, there are many obstacles to leaving:

1. Fear of leaving a situation you are used to.

2. Lack of money for alternative housing.

3. Excusing the abuser because he is not violent all the time.

4. No place to go.

5. Thinking you have no support.

6. Believing the abuser's false promise that he will change.

7. Pressure from family or friends, unaware of the abuse, for you to stay faithful to your partner and relationship.

8. Thinking abuse is OK because you saw years of domestic violence between your parents, relatives and neighbors.

9. Believing you can change the abuser's ways.

10. Feeling shame, embarrassment, guilt or emotional depression.

11. Denial that you are being abused.

12. Not wanting to leave children with the abuser.

13. Caught up in mind games of the abuser.

14. Caught in a revolving door of breaking up, making up, and unable to make that final break-up.

15. This is the only life you know, and you have been involved in a number of abusive relationships.

You can develop a plan to leave. Decide that you are a good person, worthy of respect. Decide that enough is enough; **it's over, move on.** A situation involving domestic violence does involve planning one or more ways to move on and extricate yourself from the situation. Talk to somebody about your situation: a doctor, a friend the abuser does not know, or to a hot line listed in the telephone book of an organization which shelters and counsels the abused. Have a safety plan developed with someone the abuser does not know. Take with you state identification, drivers license, birth certificate, lease or real estate deeds, money and check book. Also remember to take all your keys, medicines and medical records, address book, social security card, school records, transcripts, work permit and passport.

DUANE'S PERSONAL STORY OF A LIFE THAT ALMOST KILLED HIM:

When I first met him, he always looked down while we walked downtown. He would never look up, and I asked him why. He was a very attractive brother with light brown eyes that were always the subject of flattering comments. He told me that his ex lover thought he was persistently cruising other brothers when they were together, so he got used to looking at the ground as he walked. He shared with me how one day his ex lover hit him on the head really hard when he thought he was looking at another brother. On another day while they were at a stoplight his ex threw some soda at him and accused him of looking at a brother in the car that pulled up in the next lane of traffic. This constant mental abuse had a long term affect on him. I had to work with him to encourage him to start walking with his head held up. In time he gained the confidence needed to look at anyone he wanted to observe, whether we were together or not. After a while he was walking tall and showing everybody his beautiful smile and dreamy eyes.

Do not be like a rabbit. They spend their entire lives being silent and just when they are about to be killed, they finally scream out. Too late!

233

Chapter 22

AFTER THE LOVE HAS GONE
"KNOWING WHEN IT IS OVER"

Strong attachment is difficult -
it makes one mad or kills.

~Moroccan proverb

How many of us get stuck in love and can't move on? He has told you that he was no longer interested in being with you, or he has shown you that love has vanished. But you still want him. You want him so bad that you allow him to walk over you, and use you, just to have someone. It's over. Move on.

How many times have you been dick whipped or booty whipped, and you can't get it out of your system? It's over. Move on.

How many times have you told him to get out, don't call, and you end up calling him, begging him to come back. It's over. Move on.

How many times have you awakened in the middle of the night checking your cell, pager, and phone caller ID, hoping that he has called you, and he had not? It's over. Move on.

How many times have you driven by his house, or called his house and hung up when he picked up. Or do you show up where he goes, and sit in your car hoping to get a peek at him. It's over, move on.

How many times have you called his friends probing for information about him? How many times have you called his family members hoping that they will slip up and say something about him? It's over. Move on.

How many times have you seen him with another, or have you been told that he is with another brother, and you cry your eyes out? Did you start drinking, and doing other destructive things to you body, mind, and spirit? It's over. Move on.

Breaking up is never an easy thing. Losing someone is very difficult because the emotional pain can be overwhelming. You may spend weeks, months or even a year singing the blues.

DUANE SHARES HIS STORY.

I was in love with this brother who no longer wanted me. When I left NYC, I was leaving behind a relationship that almost caused me to spend the rest of my life in prison. I was in love. Love hurts. Love cuts deep into your soul and causes you to do stupid things. I was in love with a brother who did not love me the same way, on the same level, or with the same commitment that I gave him. That old saying, "He who loves less controls the relationship" is right on the money. I loved him more than he loved me and he used that against me. You see I really trusted this brother with my life. Whatever he wanted was ok with me. Whatever he needed, I made sure he had it. Whatever I could do to make him happy, I did for him and/or gave to him. Yet, he did not do the same for me. He used me, and then decided that he wanted someone else, a new model on the block. He wanted to move on, and get married. He told me one day that he wanted out of the relationship, and wanted us to continue to be friends. He dropped this on me when I thought that we were happy, and in love. Right in the middle of my dream, he turned it into a nightmare. With that, I was dismissed from his life. Snap, it's over, get out. Man, that felt ice cold. I hurt so badly, that I lost ten pounds in a few weeks from not wanting to eat. I took a leave of absence from my job because I cried so much that my eyes were so red, that I had to wear dark sun- glasses. That was not going to work at my place of employment. He did not want to talk to me. He had become a stranger, someone I didn't know, even though we were together for two years. I didn't know this person who got to the point of telling me that he didn't want to talk to me, or be bothered. When I look back on that period of my life, I have to shake my head and ask what in the hell was wrong with me. Not him, me. How did I let this man make me feel I was losing my fucking mind? Did I not realize I was looking and acting crazy? It was over and I didn't want to move on.

But after much prayer, and support from my friends, and months of therapy, (yes, I had to go see a shrink, and it helped) I was able to move on with my life. The lesson I learned from that experience is: never let another man have total control over your emotions, heart and feelings. Always keep some in reserve so you can fall back on them when you need to.

I thought that I never would and never could give my heart and love to another person (man or woman), but I did. I met James and we talked and I told him about the hurt I went through. He understood because he had experienced the same type of pain also. We made a promise not to do that to each other, that if we decided to move on, we would. When it is over, we would move on.

A lot of us have a "stuck on him and can't move on" story

like Duane's. You have been hurt or you are hurting today. Know that you are not alone, and you should seek professional help if you need to. It is ok, and it will help you get through this. Sometimes a simple phrase we can repeat silently in our mind again and again as an affirmation can help. A radio or television ad jingle will do. You may want to repeat and repeat silently the title or refrain of a poem or an inspirational song. Or try: "one day at a time". Or try: "keep the faith". Or try: "we shall overcome". Or try: "I will survive to see 2020". Or try: "peace be still". Or try: "that was then, this is now". Or try: "this too shall pass". The origin of the saying "this too shall pass" appears to date back to a story told about King Solomon. It is said that the King, feeling blue, asked his advisors to find him a ring he had seen in a dream. "When I feel satisfied I'm afraid it won't last. And when I don't, I am afraid my sorrow will go on forever. Find me the ring that will ease my suffering." Eventually an advisor met an old jeweler who carved into a simple gold ban the Hebrew inscription "gam zeh ya'avor" – "this too shall pass." When the King received his ring and read the inscription his sorrows turned to joy and his joy to sorrows, and then both gave way to equanimity. More recently, the saying has been popularized in the West by spiritual leaders from or inspired by the East, including: Ram Dass, the Dali Lama and Tich Nhat Hanh.

There is an old Negro spiritual, which goes: "Farther along we'll know all about it. Farther along we'll understand why. Cheer up my brother. Come live in the sunshine. We'll understand it in the sweet bye and bye".

Chapter 23

LOVING OUTSIDE THE BOX
"LEATHER 101"

Home affairs are not talked about on a public square.

~Kenyan proverb

As we reached the end of this book Duane and I had a conversation with Max about the various topics covered. Because this book is an educational and self help tool, we released our initial hesitation about giving editor Max the green light to include this topic. It is considered somewhat taboo even among some SGL people who consider themselves open-minded. Max has become a good friend and close ally of brothers and sisters in all major Black SGL community social, political, religious, academic and cultural organizations. He told us that just as each SGL person has to decide how far out of the closet he or she is going to be to str8 people: individuals in the leather community have to decide whether, when and how much of their lifestyle ought to be disclosed to SGL friends. Yes there are multiple levels of human sexuality. Many people who are not in the know may have only a vague notion of just what people in the leather community do. They may have the mistaken impression of wild, uninhibited, super freaky parties where anything goes. Fact is that the opposite is true. The more sophisticated and rare the sexual tastes and preferences, the more rigidly controlled, organized, and disciplined those activities will be.

244

Duane and me were intrigued by this unexpected revelation. We asked Max to interview a prominent member of the leather community at The Cellblock, a popular leather gay bar in Chicago. The brother was named Mr. Cellblock 2003, and gave us the following guidelines to share.

For those of you who are new to the world of BDSM, bondage, domination, sadism, masochism, what follows is the basic information. Leather, kink, fetish play are just a few of the terms used to describe the type of activity previously mentioned. I offer five pieces of advice around some of the most important elements for your new journey of discovery.

First advisory: Safe, sane and consensual (SSC)—This is the basic slogan, mantra, tenet, bedrock, cornerstone, what have you, for the BDSM community.

Safe: All activity that takes place between individuals should be conducted as safely as possible. Both individuals should leave with all general capacities and capabilities that each had before anything started between them.

Sane: Each participant should be mentally able to understand what is happening and process the impact of actions. One should be unimpaired by drugs or alcohol and capable of saying and understanding when "enough is enough."

Consensual: A mutual agreement between all parties involved is discussed and approved in regards to what the larger framework for what will happen between them consists of. If the person you have met has no idea what SSC is, or what his responsibilities are with regard to SSC, you probably don't want to or should not be having sex with that person!

Second advisory: Communicate. Talk about what you would like to experience. Talk about what you do not want to experience. Share your likes, dislikes, turn-ons, turn-offs, fantasies, boundaries, and your most bizarre, exotic, or out-there experience. It helps some one gauge just how far he can go with you, and gives a better understanding of just how far you have gone already. Let him know if he has found the right spot, if he's pushing the right button. Likewise, let him know if he has gone overboard or astray. Help him get back on track. If you are "in charge" of the scene and can't gauge how it's going, ask.

Third advisory: Educate. Education is key. BDSM is a big umbrella for a lot of smaller, loosely connected, and sometimes very highly specialized sexual activities and fetishes. Learn about those things you have an interest in. Learn the huge difference between SM and abuse. Also, learn about those areas that you have no interest in, so you are able to give an informed reason as to why you do not like something. Understand the protocol that explains why something is one particular way and not another. As a teenager at dinner time I rejected asparagus, broccoli, cauliflower and declared liver to be the most nasty of all foods. As an adult, with a desire to have nutritious, well-rounded meals, those items are on my menu often.

Fourth advisory: Explore. Give yourself permission to try something your heart desires, within the parameters of SSC. Clearly communicate with a partner who is amenable to exploring that area with you. Men have been into leather for many generations. You are not the only one with unconventional fantasies: there are others, with far greater experience, to guide you methodically and patiently at a pace comfortable to you into a transforming venture.

Fifth advisory: Travel. This could be as simple as getting out to the local leather bar, or it could be traveling to some event in another city or state. Meet people face to face. Drop your fear of self-disclosure in a safe space for thoughtful confidential conversations.

If you follow these five basic principles, you can have a good introduction to and experience with BDSM. Most people jump to the "sex play" aspect first and have to backtrack.

WHAT THE FUTURE MR. CELLBLOCK FOUND IN MATTHEW'S BASEMENT:

In March 1994 I was 22 years old and just a few months shy of graduating from college in St. Louis, MO. I'd been seriously dating Matthew for nearly two years. He was a thirty-two year old lawyer on the fast track to being named a partner in a prestigious law firm. Matthew had been flying to St. Louis, his hometown, to see me every other weekend. I was flying to New York on the alternate weekends so that we had been spending every weekend together for almost nine months at that point. I thought I knew everything about this man, but there was one thing he had not bothered to share with me, yet.

He had made veiled hints and references to "the other Matthew" that I had not met, and he said there was another "persona" to this whole, honest, man-next-door type I'd come to know, but I wrote it off. I was 22, in full control, and I knew everything, or so I thought!

Matthew was an unabashed leatherman. I found that out in his typical, grand style. One Saturday night we were in his lower west side condominium having aggressive, energetic, verbal, sweat-inducing sex. The air was filled with that intoxicating man sex smell. At some point, that session we went a little over the top, although neither of us had planned or expected for it to go there. I'd flipped Matthew onto his belly and grabbed one of his silk ties to bind his arms behind his back. He writhed, squirmed and struggled under the full weight of my naked sweaty body.

Never before in our nude wrestling had I managed to tie him up and pin him down. With one hand on his upper back, I was slapping his buns, making him groan, delighting in the feeling of power and control over him. Flipped him over one more time, mounted his chest, and with my knees on the bed on each side of his shoulder, I stroked until I ejaculated all over his face. Wow! Matthew loved that. Talk about great sex! Whew!

It took a while, but when we finally caught our breath, Matthew said, "we just did an introductory type bondage scene."

I still remember his words like they were spoken yesterday. "Bondage." "Scene." I can still remember wondering what Matthew was talking about, while laying there with a perplexed look on my face. "I love bondage," Matthew continued. "My offering of complete control of the situation, my total submission to you is a huge turn-on for me, and you took to it like a duck to water," he added. "Control." "Submission." I can distinctly remember asking myself the question: What in the world was he talking about?

"You have been coming here for nine months, and you've never been down to my basement," said Matthew. He continued, "At this time I think you should see what is down there."

Curiosity is said to have killed the cat. I was filled with nine lives worth of curiosity, and lots of questions. Terminology was being thrown about that I didn't quite understand. Matthew was talking very cryptically. What was all this stuff about his basement?   Seeking answers I got off the bed, slowly walked through the kitchen, opened the door and step by step, went down the stairs that led to his basement. The lights were off, and it was completely dark. He had painted the walls black. I could make out the lone light bulb above the bottom step, and reached out to pull the string to turn it on. I was unprepared for the sight that began just a few feet in front of me.

A leather hammock? (sling) Chains dangling from the ceiling. A big stand in the shape of an "X"? Rope. Handcuffs. Hanging on a towel rack on the wall were five handkerchiefs in gray, light blue, yellow, fuschia and olive. Saran Wrap. Blindfolds. Tape. Mirrors everywhere.

"Welcome to my dungeon," Matthew said, startling me, as he walked up behind me silently in bare feet. "All this is part of that other persona I kept mentioning to you," he continued. "I'm a guy into leather, and this is my play space, and these are my toys and gear.

My head was swimming. The air was electric. I did not know what to think. A bit of fear struck, and I thought about leaving, more specifically running out of there! As I looked around the room, however, I calmed down, and became more curious about all the things I saw. Is that a steel cage over there? I found myself wondering. What is this? And what could that possibly be used for? I looked more closely at a stack of VHS tapes. "Wanted Bondage Trainee", "Bondage Trio", "Bondage Memories", "More Guys in Bondage." I grabbed one of the tapes and put it into the VCR. Matthew turned on the television. We watched a bit of it, neither of us talking. Matthew just stared at me, trying to gauge my reaction. I was trying to focus on the movie. What did all this mean? What was Matthew telling me? I didn't get an answer watching the video, but it did arouse me. Matthew clearly saw that. We both got up and headed back upstairs to talk about this new area of exploration for the two of us.

Chapter 24

LOOKING FOR A NEW LOVE
"AND BEING CONTENT BY YOURSELF"

The hunter in pursuit of an elephant does not stop to throw stones at birds.

~Ugandan proverb

Life is short and then you die.

What we all need to realize is that we only get one life. I read somewhere that life is not a rehearsal and you do not get a second chance. You only get one chance at this beautiful gift. So, live your life to its fullest. Give it all you got. Just read your daily paper and see that young men are dying of AIDS, dropping dead of heart attacks while they are in their early 30's. People just going to work, only to end up dead because of an act of random gun violence and they were in the wrong place at the wrong time. Tomorrow is not promised to any of us. Treat people the way you want to be treated, be honest with yourself, and show some love to everyone you pass on the street. When you have on your fly gear, and know that you are looking good and fabulous, and you step over and around another brother just because he has not arrived. Stop, at least a smile and a hello won't hurt you, and just might make his day.

One of the biggest issues that I have about the life style is that we can too often be the most-unfriendly group of men on this planet. That is one reason why I rarely go to clubs and other gay events. Not enough people speak or go out of their way to make an introduction. There could be more exchanges of business cards and more networking. Many middle class African-American SGL men just need to drop that defensive elitist attitude like a hot potato. Does that come from a basic inner insecurity? We can be so judgmental about everything. We think that if we are not perfect, then others will know it and talk about us. That lowers feelings of self-esteem throughout the community of "family". We compare our bodies with others, and spend years and thousands of dollars at a gym trying to get something that we want just to make others desire us (see chapter 13. **No fats No fems**). We take our last few dollars to buy the latest designer clothes to attend the "must be seen at" party, knowing that we don't have a penny in the bank and still living at our parents house (in the basement). We lie about our age, our work, or education, or dick size, how many sex partners we have had, (or how many we have not had), how many hearts we have broken, and the list goes on and on.

Young SGL brothers are lost. In my personal opinion, they have far too few visible and affirming role models to follow. A lot of the young SGL brothers are learning from each other what older wiser brothers ought to teach them of what is expected when you are a SGL. That is why so many of them are getting infected with the HIV virus and other STDs because they don't know what is real, and what is a game.

The last time I stepped out to a club or a party to just be out: I thought I was attending an elementary school reunion. The boys were so undisiplined and so flamboyant. They had lost every ounce of their masculinity, or were serving attitude with arched eyebrows and glossed over lips. Perhaps the key to personal and community growth and development is to make a commitment to make ourselves: to become stronger internally first, to be concerned with cosmetic externals last.

WORKING OUT TO STAY AND KEEP FIT

In this lifestyle it seems that brothers spend all of their time at the gym. Gyms and health clubs have become places of meeting other men for getting dates, socializing and networking. Every year so many of us make resolutions pertaining to getting back into the gym or losing weight. Most of us only work hard at this so we can stay in the game, or attract men, or wear those outfits that only men with the right body can wear.

We feel that working out and staying in shape should be a personal goal, and not attached to finding a man. If you only are working out or spending thousands of dollars for a health club member to find or keep a man, then that is the wrong motivation.

I can remember one year that I hired a personal trainer and went to the gym everyday and hated it. I only did it because I wanted to work the nerves of the brothers that summer. I would have to force myself to go see my trainer. He would cuss me out when I would not give him 100%. He would call me fat pig, and sloppy hog. It was his way to get me to work out and not play. He wanted me to take his job seriously.

One day when I showed up at the gym, instead of my regular trainer, there was another brother filling in for him. This bro was 6'4", dreads, light eyes, and a body that would make a dead man come back to life and feel horny.

He was so good looking that it made me sweat and I had not even started working out. His name was Ty and he was very nice. He read my file and said that I needed to work on my upper body today. He directed me on the routine that he wanted me to do. While he was standing over me, I looked up and saw that he had a hard on print in his tight white biker shorts. It was very clear that bro man was hard as steel. He didn't try to hide it; he just took over me and directed me to what he wanted me to do. When I was finished with those sets and stood up, I couldn't help but look at his erection. He caught my eyes and said, "this comes from working out outside of the gym", and started laughing. Then he said if you want to see what type of exercise that I do for this (pointing at his hot rod) call me later. I was ready to go after that conversation. I had really been worked.

I called him and after a brief conversation he told me that the only reason that he had become a personal trainer was to meet brothers. That the gym is the best place to meet men. He said that he has made a lot of money from brothers who are not serious about working out, but they needed to. He said that if men would not try to get in

260

shape for others but for themselves then they could stick to the program and get their monies worth.

After that, I decided that I would work out for no one but me. I would try to get a six pack and firm pecs for no one but me. I would not spend money I didn't have for a high priced gym membership just to show off. I would utilize the YMCA and outdoor free activities to take care of my body. I developed the following 10 rules for me that might work for you:

1. Make working out a necessity in your life.

2. Keep it simple.

3. Set Realistic Achievable goals.

4. Chart your progress.

5. Go one on one.

6. Hang in there even when you want to give up

7. Miss a day of working out, re motivate yourself

8. Relax and feel better. Get rid of the stress and tension in your life.

9. Get a personal trainer only if you can afford one and you need help.

10. Place pictures of how you want to look all over your
house....great motivation!

SGL RESOURCES
INFORMATIONAL WEBSITES

Blacklist **http://www.blackstripe.com/blacklist/** has news and information affecting lesbian, gay, bisexual and transgendered people of African descent. Also has biographical information on black lesbians and gays.

American Civil Liberties Union's Gay Lesbian Rights Page **http://www.aclu.org/issues/gav/hmgl.html** has excellent list of resources, news, and action taken by the ACLU organized subjects.

Assault on Gay America

http://www.pbs.org/wgbh/pages/frontline/shows/assualt/ by Frontline, analyzes the death of Billy Jack Gaither, historians and psychologists discussion on gay attitudes and hatred, Bible scholars interpretation of Scripture, scientific research, and cultural history.

Human Rights Campaign **http://www.hrc.org** has resources for coming out, finding LGBT-friendly workplaces, marriages/civil unions, children and adoption information, and legal information.

Pridenet: Worldwide Gay Lesbian Transgender and Bisexual Resources **http://www.pridenet.com/** has all variety of support and resources organized by states and countries.

K. Godfrey Easter is a social activist, engaging public speaker, and the author of LOVE LIFTED ME: In Spite of The Church. **http://www.loveliftedmenetwork.com**

Black, Gay & Chrristian: An Inspirational Guidebook to Daily Living **http://groups.yahoo.com/group/BlackGayChristian/**

Adodi is a support group of SGL men of African ancestry with affiliates in several cities and an on-line discussion group MenofAdodi@Yahoogroups.com

Man2Man Alliance **http://www.man2manalliance.org/** A group which promotes the emotional intensity and erotic power of frottage, while encouraging the avoidance of all anal sex.

Service members Legal Defense Network **http://www.sldn.org/**

site has news, legal information and publications useful for military personnel who are dealing with the "don't ask, don't tell" policy.

National Gay and Lesbian Task Force
http://www.ngltf.org/ a national organization working for the civil rights advocacy of gay, lesbian, bisexual and transgendered. Site has news, opinion, publications, event information, and advocacy information.

OutProud **http://www.outproud.org/** has a wide range of resources for youth and educators from articles, school resources, online brochures, internet survey results, bulletin boards, and bibliography of useful print resources.

Parents and Friends of Lesbians, Gay, Bisexual, and Transgendered Persons **http://www.pflag.org/** site has local chapters, has educational resources for families, support information, and advocacy information.

www.keithboykin.com Keith Boykin provides daily information on SGL news worldwide.

Centers for Disease Control National AIDS Hotline
1-800-342-AIDS   www.cdc.gov/hiv

www.cdcnip.org

www.blackAIDSDAY.org

www.redcross.org

www.gmad.org

www.balmingilead.org

www.blca.org

www.ushelpingus.org

Final thoughts from the Author
James Williams

Writing this guide has brought my partner and me closer together. It made us take a look at our past, present and future. There were times as we both read each other's stories and opinions that we wanted to get angry and question something that we didn't know about. There are one or two chapters where I was writing about my experiences and he questioned me about my intentions. I told him in the beginning that I wanted to be open and honest about my experience in the life so another brother won't have to go through what I did. That is why we originally titled this: **Staying Power - An Unofficial Guide to Developing Positive African-American MSM Relationships**.

We wanted to put out something that would be of help to others.

We hope you may use this work as a guide referring back time and time again as you move through your romantic encounters. We don't claim to know all the answers—we only wanted to provide a few answers to the questions of Black SGL love.

MESSAGE FROM THE PUBLISHER

Chicago Moon Publishing, Inc. was created to give writers an opportunity to get work published. I know that there are many SGL men and women who are talented writers who have expressed their feelings about love and life on napkins, in journals and on sheets of paper that never get to be shared with others. I have attended many open mic events and have been blown awy with the way that these individuals can speak words, phrases, and emotions free styling. I wanted to give these individuals a way to follow their dreams and see their work become a published book. Then the world can read these works of art.

All of my staff are proud of this book. It took over 16 months to get into your hands. Through the ups and downs the author, editor and staf worked together like one fine-tuned machine to complete this mission. As the founder, publisher and CEO of Chciago Moon Publishing, Inc. I invite you to contact me if you have a manuscript or an idea for a book. If you are ready to move ahead and get your work published I welcome your submissions, and look forward to meeting and working with you.

I also invite you to give me your feedback on STAYING POWER. There will be a STAYING POWER 2, and your input might be used.

May you always have love in your life.

Sincerely,

James L. King
Publisher and CEO

SPECIAL THANKS

SPECIAL THANKS TO THE FOLLOWING PEOPLE:

To the staff at Chicago Moon Publishing. Otis Richardson for your illustrations, you rock, dude. Tim McGuire of GO design for your skills in laying out this book. Pierre Cameron for taking the beautiful cover photo. Merritt Franklin, Van Rountree, U. "Pete" Peterson, Jeff Alston, Tyrone Fowler, Will Lewis, Trenton Edmonds, M. Douglas, Dr. K Harold Smith, Omari and Steve for being so damn sexy of the cover. And for the many cups of coffee at Starbucks that kept us all going. We would like to thank everybody who was interviewed or provided information to us for this project. Thanks to individuals who provided support, and shared their stories of love. A special thanks goes out to Andre Holmes who was the first editor. And above all others, thanks be to God who is the head of all our lives.

ACKNOWLEDGMENTS

We would like to thank all of the individuals who shared their experiences, memories, ups and downs for this book.

We also thank our ex lovers, trade, hustlers and all the other men who helped shape our thoughts and feelings about loving a Black man.

We would like to thank the editors whose touch made it a book that we are very proud of.

We also would like to thank you for purchasing this book. Follow your dreams; they do come true.

We also give a special thank you to Chicago Moon Publishing Inc. With out your vision, we would still be trying to get this done. Thank you from the bottom of our hearts. Black business is a beautiful thing.

STAYING POWER

Mail Check or Money Order to:

Chicago Moon Publishing Co.

P.O. Box 804902 Chicago, IL 60680

Email: chicagomoonpub@aol.com

Web site: www.chicagomoonpub.com

Date_____

Name_____

Address_____

City_____ _State_____Zip Code_____

Number of books ordered_____ Total Cost $_____

Shipping & handling is 15% of total # ordered

$_____

Total amount due $_____

__ Check   __ Money Order

__ Visa   __ Mastercard

Expiration Date:_____

Card #_____

Driver's License #_____

P.O.#_____

Signature:_____

Date:_____

ABOUT THE EDITOR

Max Smith:

Born in Hickory, North Carolina, graduated Jefferson City (Missouri) Senior High School, Michigan State University B.A. 1976 Communication Arts. Employed in various automotive sales and management positions. Life-long cultural, social and political activist: who worked with Illinois Gay Rights Task Force, organized Chicago chapter National Coalition of Black Lesbians and Gays. 1991 inductee into the City of Chicago's Gay and Lesbian Hall of Fame. Recent service on the Adodi Chicago Steering Committee. Columnist with IDENTITY magazine, and Windy City Times newspaper.